Joyce Appleby on *Thomas Jefferson*
Louis Auchincloss on *Theodore Roosevelt*
Jean H. Baker on *James Buchanan*
H. W. Brands on *Woodrow Wilson*
Alan Brinkley on *John F. Kennedy*
Douglas Brinkley on *Gerald R. Ford*
Josiah Bunting III on *Ulysses S. Grant*
James MacGregor Burns and Susan Dunn on *George Washington*
Charles W. Calhoun on *Benjamin Harrison*
Gail Collins on *William Henry Harrison*
Robert Dallek on *Harry S. Truman*
John W. Dean on *Warren G. Harding*
John Patrick Diggins on *John Adams*
Elizabeth Drew on *Richard M. Nixon*
John S. D. Eisenhower on *Zachary Taylor*
Paul Finkelman on *Millard Fillmore*
Annette Gordon-Reed on *Andrew Johnson*
Henry F. Graff on *Grover Cleveland*
David Greenberg on *Calvin Coolidge*
Gary Hart on *James Monroe*
Michael F. Holt on *Franklin Pierce*
Roy Jenkins on *Franklin Delano Roosevelt*
Zachary Karabell on *Chester Alan Arthur*
Lewis H. Lapham on *William Howard Taft*
William E. Leuchtenburg on *Herbert Hoover*
Gary May on *John Tyler*
George McGovern on *Abraham Lincoln*
Timothy Naftali on *George H. W. Bush*
Charles Peters on *Lyndon B. Johnson*
Kevin Phillips on *William McKinley*
Robert V. Remini on *John Quincy Adams*
Ira Rutkow on *James A. Garfield*
John Seigenthaler on *James K. Polk*
Hans L. Trefousse on *Rutherford B. Hayes*
Tom Wicker on *Dwight D. Eisenhower*
Ted Widmer on *Martin Van Buren*
Sean Wilentz on *Andrew Jackson*
Garry Wills on *James Madison*
Julian E. Zelizer on *Jimmy Carter*

Lyndon B. Johnson

Charles Peters

Lyndon B. Johnson

THE AMERICAN PRESIDENTS

ARTHUR M. SCHLESINGER, JR., AND SEAN WILENTZ

GENERAL EDITORS

Times Books

HENRY HOLT AND COMPANY, NEW YORK

Times Books
Henry Holt and Company, LLC
Publishers since 1866
175 Fifth Avenue
New York, New York 10010
www.henryholt.com

Henry Holt® is a registered trademark of
Henry Holt and Company, LLC.

Library of Congress Cataloging-in-Publication Data

Peters, Charles, 1926–
 Lyndon B. Johnson / Charles Peters; Arthur M. Schlesinger, Jr., and Sean
Wilentz, general editors.—1st ed.
   p. cm.—(The American presidents)
 Includes bibliographical references and index.
 ISBN 978-0-8050-8239-5
 1. Johnson, Lyndon B. (Lyndon Baines), 1908–1973. 2. United States—
Politics and government—1945–1989. 3. Presidents—United States—
Biography. I. Schlesinger, Arthur M. (Arthur Meier), 1917–2007.
II. Wilentz, Sean. III. Title.
 E847.P48 2010
 973.923092—dc22
 [B]   2009045612

First Edition 2010

Printed in the United States of America
 1 3 5 7 9 10 8 6 4 2

With gratitude and affection for all those who
helped create and sustain the Washington Monthly

Contents

Editor's Note

THE AMERICAN PRESIDENCY

The president is the central player in the American political order. That would seem to contradict the intentions of the Founding Fathers. Remembering the horrid example of the British monarchy, they invented a separation of powers in order, as Justice Brandeis later put it, "to preclude the exercise of arbitrary power." Accordingly, they divided the government into three allegedly equal and coordinate branches—the executive, the legislative, and the judiciary.

But a system based on the tripartite separation of powers has an inherent tendency toward inertia and stalemate. One of the three branches must take the initiative if the system is to move. The executive branch alone is structurally capable of taking that initiative. The Founders must have sensed this when they accepted Alexander Hamilton's proposition in the Seventieth Federalist that "energy in the executive is a leading character in the definition of good government." They thus envisaged a strong president—but within an equally strong system of constitutional accountability. (The term *imperial presidency* arose in the 1970s to describe the situation when the balance between power and accountability is upset in favor of the executive.)

The American system of self-government thus comes to focus in the presidency—"the vital place of action in the system," as Woodrow Wilson put it. Henry Adams, himself the great-grandson and grandson of presidents as well as the most brilliant of American historians, said that the American president "resembles the commander of a ship at sea. He must have a helm to grasp, a course to steer, a port to seek." The men in the White House (thus far only men, alas) in steering their chosen courses have shaped our destiny as a nation.

Biography offers an easy education in American history, rendering the past more human, more vivid, more intimate, more accessible, more connected to ourselves. Biography reminds us that presidents are not supermen. They are human beings too, worrying about decisions, attending to wives and children, juggling balls in the air, and putting on their pants one leg at a time. Indeed, as Emerson contended, "There is properly no history; only biography."

Presidents serve us as inspirations, and they also serve us as warnings. They provide bad examples as well as good. The nation, the Supreme Court has said, has "no right to expect that it will always have wise and humane rulers, sincerely attached to the principles of the Constitution. Wicked men, ambitious of power, with hatred of liberty and contempt of law, may fill the place once occupied by Washington and Lincoln."

The men in the White House express the ideals and the values, the frailties and the flaws, of the voters who send them there. It is altogether natural that we should want to know more about the virtues and the vices of the fellows we have elected to govern us. As we know more about them, we will know more about ourselves. The French political philosopher Joseph de Maistre said, "Every nation has the government it deserves."

At the start of the twenty-first century, forty-two men have made it to the Oval Office. (George W. Bush is counted our forty-third president, because Grover Cleveland, who served nonconsecutive terms, is counted twice.) Of the parade of presidents, a dozen or so lead the polls periodically conducted by historians and political scientists. What makes a great president?

Great presidents possess, or are possessed by, a vision of an ideal America. Their passion, as they grasp the helm, is to set the ship of state on the right course toward the port they seek. Great presidents also have a deep psychic connection with the needs, anxieties, dreams of people. "I do not believe," said Wilson, "that any man can lead who does not act . . . under the impulse of a profound sympathy with those whom he leads—a sympathy which is insight—an insight which is of the heart rather than of the intellect."

"All of our great presidents," said Franklin D. Roosevelt, "were leaders of thought at a time when certain ideas in the life of the nation had to be clarified." So Washington incarnated the idea of federal union, Jefferson and Jackson the idea of democracy, Lincoln union and freedom, Cleveland rugged honesty. Theodore Roosevelt and Wilson, said FDR, were both "moral leaders, each in his own way and his own time, who used the presidency as a pulpit."

To succeed, presidents not only must have a port to seek but they must convince Congress and the electorate that it is a port worth seeking. Politics in a democracy is ultimately an educational process, an adventure in persuasion and consent. Every president stands in Theodore Roosevelt's bully pulpit.

The greatest presidents in the scholars' rankings, Washington, Lincoln, and Franklin Roosevelt, were leaders who confronted and overcame the republic's greatest crises. Crisis widens presidential opportunities for bold and imaginative action. But it does not guarantee presidential greatness. The crisis of secession did not spur Buchanan or the crisis of depression spur

Hoover to creative leadership. Their inadequacies in the face of crisis allowed Lincoln and the second Roosevelt to show the difference individuals make to history. Still, even in the absence of first-order crisis, forceful and persuasive presidents—Jefferson, Jackson, James K. Polk, Theodore Roosevelt, Harry Truman, John F. Kennedy, Ronald Reagan, George W. Bush—are able to impose their own priorities on the country.

The diverse drama of the presidency offers a fascinating set of tales. Biographies of American presidents constitute a chronicle of wisdom and folly, nobility and pettiness, courage and cunning, forthrightness and deceit, quarrel and consensus. The turmoil perennially swirling around the White House illuminates the heart of the American democracy.

It is the aim of the American Presidents series to present the grand panorama of our chief executives in volumes compact enough for the busy reader, lucid enough for the student, authoritative enough for the scholar. Each volume offers a distillation of character and career. I hope that these lives will give readers some understanding of the pitfalls and potentialities of the presidency and also of the responsibilities of citizenship. Truman's famous sign—"The buck stops here"—tells only half the story. Citizens cannot escape the ultimate responsibility. It is in the voting booth, not on the presidential desk, that the buck finally stops.

—Arthur M. Schlesinger, Jr.

Lyndon B. Johnson

1

Early Life

When Lyndon Baines Johnson entered this life on August 27, 1908, rural America was a vastly different place than it is today. Although motor cars had begun to appear in cities, the horse and buggy provided the only means of transportation in the countryside. Passenger trains traveling over a rail network much more extensive than today's did give many rural Americans access to cities and the business, cultural, and educational opportunities they offered. But there was no train service to Hye or Stonewall, the tiny communities between which was located the farm on the banks of the Pedernales River where Lyndon Johnson was born to Samuel Ealy Johnson and Rebekah Baines Johnson.

Reaching the nearest city of any size, Austin, required at least two days on dirt roads that turned into impassable quagmires when it rained. The trip gradually became less arduous as Henry Ford's Model T, first introduced the year Lyndon was born, gradually became rural America's preferred means of transportation, a role in which it was firmly established by the early 1920s.

Otherwise, life on the farm was largely devoid of modern conveniences. Rural roads did not get paved until the late 1920s and 1930s, when electricity also began to become available. Clothes were washed by hand with water drawn from wells. The outhouse was far more common than in-house plumbing. At night, light came from kerosene lamps. Meals were cooked on woodstoves with lunch, usually called dinner, the main meal of the day. (What we would today call dinner was referred to as supper.) There was, of course, no vacuum cleaner. Sweeping had to be done with brooms. Sweeping, carrying in wood and water, cooking over hot woodstoves, and scrubbing clothes on washboards in tin tubs made a hard life for women like Rebekah Johnson.

Sam and Rebekah were—or at least thought of themselves as—a cut above the usual run of country folk. Sam had already been elected to the Texas legislature and was concluding his second term when Lyndon was born. Rebekah had graduated from Baylor University at a time when college was beyond the reach of most American women and practically all of those living on a farm. Lyndon liked to brag, "My ancestors were teachers and lawyers and college presidents and governors when the Kennedys in this country were still tending bar." He would also boast about the rugged pioneers in his background, with tales of fighting Indians, herding cattle all the way through Kansas, and—displaying the gift for embroidering fact that would become characteristic—family members martyred at the Alamo. His mother, however, was more interested in the genteel than the pioneer side of the family background. This concern made her come close to turning her child into what other boys would call a sissy.

Years later, Lyndon recalled, "one of the first things I remember about my daddy was the time he cut my hair. When I was four or five I had long curls. He hated them. 'He's a boy!' he'd say to my mother. 'And you're making a sissy of him. You've got to cut those curls.' My mother refused. Then one Sunday morn-

ing when she went off to church, he took the big scissors and
cut off all my hair. When my mother came home, she refused to
speak to him for a week."

When Johnson was eight, he made clear he shared his father's
concern by stopping the violin and dancing lessons his mother
had arranged. His mother reacted just as she had to the haircut:
"For days after I quit those lessons, she walked around the
house pretending I was dead."

His mother's conditional love seems to have affected Johnson in two ways. First, he always worried that whatever approval
he might receive could be quickly withdrawn. And second, he
imitated his mother in his relationships with others, offering
generous love until the recipient disappointed him and then
administering to that unfortunate soul "the Johnson freeze-
out," the same treatment his mother had given him.

Johnson had an idealized view of his mother, describing her
as "sweet" and "gentle." "A more accurate description," according to George Reedy, who got to know Rebekah after he joined
Johnson's Senate staff, "would include such adjectives as tough,
stern, unyielding, obstinate, domineering. She was an unrelent-
ing snob who reminded everyone in the first few minutes of a
meeting that her ancestry included high-ranking Baptist clerics
and intellectuals."

As he grew older, Lyndon was fascinated by the political
world in which his father dwelt. When Lyndon was ten, in
1918, Sam was again elected to the Texas legislature. In the
next six years, Lyndon often accompanied his father to the legislative chamber in Austin. Fascinated by the proceedings on the
floor, he watched for hours and then wandered through the
halls, soaking up the backstage gossip. Though a so-so student
in school, Lyndon proved to be what one of his father's colleagues described as a "very bright and alert" observer of legislative wheeling and dealing.

Lyndon also loved the constant campaigning that was necessary to preserve his father's seat. "We drove in the Model T Ford
from farm to farm, up and down the valley, stopping at every
door," he would recall. "My father would do most of the talking.
He would bring the neighbors up to date on local gossip, talk
about the crops and about the bills he'd introduced in the
legislature. . . . Christ, sometimes I wished it could go on for-
ever."

Sam's love of politics and his hatred of bigotry—he took on
the Ku Klux Klan when it still dominated Texas—made a lasting impact on his son. But Sam also endowed Lyndon with
something considerably less desirable, a taste for alcohol. Sam
drank too much, and his drinking caused continuing tension in
his marriage. This was the age of the Woman's Christian Tem-
perance Union, the movement that led the nation to amend its
constitution in 1919 to prohibit the consumption and sale of
alcoholic beverages. The movement, though fueled by the many
domestic tragedies brought about by excessive drinking, had
at its core an unattractive self-righteousness, which Rebekah
brought in full measure to her relationship with Sam. She
would enlist Lyndon in denouncing his father's unfortunate
habit. As in most such cases in that era, there was a lot of anger
accompanied by little attempt to understand the problem. The
result was that Sam continued drinking and, with no one to
figure out why, Lyndon, who had berated his father for his bad
habit, became in adulthood a heavy drinker himself.

When Lyndon finished high school in Johnson City, where
the family had moved, his mother wanted him to go to college,
but he rebelled. He wanted to go to California with some friends.
He was at an age when young people flirt with the hope of
something magical happening to them that will give them the
success their parents had to work so hard to grab even a piece of.
And for Americans the one place that symbolized the possibility

of that magic actually occurring was the Golden State of California. As was the case with many other young dreamers, however, that magic didn't happen to Lyndon Johnson. After a series of odd jobs, he returned home sixteen months later and worked for more than a year on road construction near his home.

He then followed his mother's wishes and enrolled at the Southwest Texas State Teachers College in San Marcos, about thirty miles from Johnson City. San Marcos, as the college was often called, had seven hundred students, all white and nearly all Christian.

Few of the students were wealthy. Indeed, one of the school's attractions was that it was sufficiently inexpensive to be affordable, if only barely, by most Texas families. Tuition was seventeen dollars a semester, and room and board could be had for less than thirty dollars a month. Still, the Johnsons were sufficiently impecunious that Lyndon had to work to supplement what his family could pay.

He got a job as a kind of gofer for the school's president, Cecil Evans, delivering messages to the faculty in an era when telephones were still not in every office. In this role, Johnson displayed the gift for sycophancy that was to prove so valuable for him in later life. His flattery of Evans was shameless—and it had the predictable effect: "I was tremendously fond of him," Evans said. Lyndon became so influential with Evans that he was soon accompanying the president on trips to Austin, where Evans lobbied for financial help for his college.

Another patron and mentor whose favor Johnson sought was Professor Harry Greene, a professor of government. In Greene's case, as indeed for many of those who played a similar role in Johnson's life, genuine affection and respect were as much a factor in Johnson's sycophancy as his desire to use the mentor to further his own career. "A cross between Thomas Jefferson and Robert LaFollette" is the way one Johnson biographer describes

Greene, "a great respecter of democracy and the Bill of Rights and a self-appointed champion of the common man"—which actually turned out to be a pretty good description of the man his pupil Lyndon Johnson would become.

And, of course, Johnson fully shared Greene's passion for politics. One classmate recalls how Lyndon regaled his friends with what one described as "marathon talk about political personalities and how he would run a campaign if he were a candidate." Lyndon, who was six feet three by the time he reached San Marcos, was skinny during his college years. This tall and lanky young man walking, according to a friend, "with long, loping strides," rushed around the campus "like the seat of his britches was on fire," managing always to look busy—indeed, "he could look busy doing nothing."

Johnson's ambition and potential were clear to all. He "was going somewhere," as they said. But, though they liked his warmth, his interest in them, and his ability to entertain, they disliked his bragging, his "brown nosing," and how "he'd just interrupt you" and insist on dominating the conversation.

He was popular enough to be named summer editor of the college newspaper and to play a major role in winning the student body presidency for his friend Willard Deason. He even managed to do something he was never able to do as president: suppress an article making fun of him that had been written for the college paper.

Like Franklin Roosevelt, who was blackballed by the Porcellian Club at Harvard, Johnson was blackballed by the Black Stars, who at the time were the most powerful group on campus. During his college years he also ultimately suffered rejection by Carol Davis, a pretty blonde with whom he had fallen in love and courted for over a year. Carol was the daughter of a prosperous businessman who regarded Johnson's family as "shiftless dirt farmers and grubby politicians." Carol may have been the girl of Lyndon's dreams, but he was fortunate to have escaped having Mr. Davis as a father-in-law—Davis was a right-winger and a member of the Ku Klux Klan.

Just before their relationship ended, Carol and Lyndon attended the 1928 Democratic National Convention, which was held in Houston that year. Johnson used his college editor-ship to gain press credentials and was able to get on the floor where he could rub elbows with the party's movers and shakers. He got to see Franklin Roosevelt place in nomination the Happy Warrior, Alfred E. Smith, who became the convention's choice to be the Democratic candidate for president.

Following the convention Johnson spent what would have been his senior year at San Marcos teaching students in the small town of Cotulla. He took the teaching job because he needed the money to pay for his senior year at San Marcos.

If you were to take the train on the old Missouri Pacific line from San Antonio south to Laredo, you would encounter some of the flattest, driest, most inhospitable country in the United States. Along about halfway, Lyndon Johnson found Cotulla, a small town divided by the railroad tracks into one community that was Anglo and another that was Mexican American. Most of the Mexicans were poor farmworkers, treated by the Anglos, Lyndon said, "just worse than you'd treat a dog," and segregated in theaters, restaurants, and schools. It was to the Mexican school that Johnson was assigned.

The challenge brought out his very best. And a formidable challenge it was. His pupils lived in shanties, without running water, electricity, or plumbing. Some were so hungry that John-son once saw them "going through a garbage pile shaking the coffee grounds from grapefruit rinds and sucking the rinds for the juice." But the school itself was decently housed in a brick building, although it was surrounded by a barren playground devoid of swings, slides, seesaws, or any of the other apparatus to which most schoolchildren were accustomed.

Johnson's class consisted of twenty-eight fifth, sixth, seventh, and eighth graders, many of whom were barely literate. The other teachers at the school, white women, made a quick exit at the end of the school day, not being eager to mix with the students more than they had to. Johnson, however, came early and left late. Determined to inspire a sense of hope in the beaten-down children, he developed extracurricular activities and arranged a parent-teacher group. He held spelling bees and organized a band, a debate club, and baseball and softball games. "I took my first paycheck and bought them a net, singing books for the choir, and second-hand musical instruments," he recalled. One check may not have bought all that, but there is no question that Lyndon Johnson had an impact on the children of Cotulla.

"His being there," one student said, was "like a blessing from the clear sky." Another described him as "the kind of teacher you wanted to work for." The general feeling was that he had helped them "tremendously."

Johnson had not taken the job in Cotulla to do good but to make money. Nevertheless, he had done good, and the experience left an indelible impression on his mind. "You never forgot what poverty and hatred could do, when you see the scars on the hopeful face of a young child," he said. "They never seem to know why people dislike them. But they knew it was so, because I saw it in their eyes."

The impact of the experience is suggested by the fact that Johnson uttered those words thirty-six years later, speaking in behalf of the Voting Rights Act of 1965.

The Cotulla School District was so impressed by Johnson— "one of the very best men I've ever had," said the superintendent— that he was implored to remain as one of its teachers. But

Lyndon felt it was time to leave. "I wanted to finish my college work and in June of '29 I went back to San Marcos and continued right straight through there until August of 1930 when I got a bachelor of science degree," he later explained.

During that winter, Lyndon and his friend Vernon Whiteside visited the family home in Johnson City. Sam Johnson's attempts at making a living outside of politics—he had lost his legislative seat in 1924—had largely failed, and the family was living at the poverty level. "What we had for supper that night was cornbread and milk," Whiteside said. Seeing his mother cook over a woodstove, Johnson determined that one of his aims in life would be to make sure that the Hill Country got electricity.

Nineteen-thirty was an election year, activating Lyndon's passion for politics. He worked for Welly Hopkins, who was running for the state senate, and his energy and intelligence quickly succeeded in impressing the candidate. "I rode all the byways in Blanco County with Lyndon," said Hopkins, "and followed his judgment in Hays County almost completely because he had a favorable standing with the local people in San Marcos."

While working for Hopkins and finishing his senior year at San Marcos, Johnson asked his uncle George Johnson, who was chairman of the history department at Sam Houston High School, to help him get a teaching job in Houston. Uncle George came through, securing Lyndon a job teaching public speaking and business arithmetic at Sam Houston.

Lyndon threw himself into his new assignment with characteristic vigor. One of his colleagues described him working "as if his life depended on it."

But a life-changing event interrupted Lyndon's teaching career. The congressman from the congressional district that included San Marcos and the Johnson home in Blanco County died in 1931, and a special election was scheduled to replace him. One of the candidates was a rich Texan named Richard

Kleberg. Among those whose support Kleberg sought were Welly Hopkins, whose campaign Lyndon had helped, and Sam Johnson, who retained political influence in his county. When Kleberg won, Welly and Sam recommended Lyndon to be Kleberg's secretary, which was what today's staff director was called back when there was very little staff to direct.

On the day Kleberg called Sam Houston High School to offer Lyndon the job, a colleague described his reaction: "He turned to me and said with great excitement, 'Mr. Kleberg wants me to be his private secretary. I'll have to go up and tell Uncle George,'" who after all had gotten Lyndon the teaching position and whose approval he needed. Uncle George—who had once told a young friend, "If I were a young man like you, I'd run for Congress"—most definitely approved. Johnson accepted the appointment.

2

Mr. Johnson Comes
to Washington

When people come to Washington to work in the government, they rarely need to reside there for longer than six months before they are infected by what has come to be called Potomac Fever. The principal symptom of this malady is a resolve to find a way to stay in Washington, and, if required to leave, to return as soon as possible.

Lyndon Johnson first arrived in Washington on December 7, 1931. He managed to stay for all but two of the next thirty-seven years.

Traveling in style with his new boss, the wealthy Texas congressman Richard Kleberg, Johnson slept in what for a rural Texan must have been the luxury of a Pullman car. Emerging from Union Station, there smack in front of him was the Capitol building. One can imagine how that sight must have stirred his soul. From there, he and Kleberg went directly to the May-flower Hotel, one of the city's best and home to several prominent senators and congressmen. For his first few days, Johnson stayed in Kleberg's suite, drinking in the hotel's heady mixture of power and elegance.

Then Johnson moved to considerably less exalted quarters in the basement of the Dodge Hotel on Capitol Hill. The Dodge, while definitely not the Mayflower, had its own attractions; the other residents consisted of a high proportion of congressional staff members. They offered Johnson the chance to forge valuable connections. It was an opportunity the young Texan seized by the lapels. He quickly got to know the other residents, taking every opening to start a conversation, even while shaving and showering in the basement community bathroom.

For Johnson, Capitol Hill in 1931 provided considerably more fertile networking territory than the executive branch of government, which was headed by a Republican president, Herbert Hoover, and a cabinet featuring patricians like Secretary of State Henry Stimson and Secretary of the Treasury Andrew Mellon. Few in this conservative administration were likely to feel instant rapport with a Texas populist.

But on the Hill, Johnson's new friends included not just staff members but actual congressmen. He cultivated three rising stars in the Texas delegation: the widely respected Sam Rayburn, the populist Wright Patman, and, later, the very progressive Maury Maverick, whose populism was even more ardent than Patman's. Rayburn, a bachelor, soon began to look on Johnson as a son. Once when Lyndon was enduring a bad bout of pneumonia, he woke up to find Rayburn sitting by his bed. When Johnson asked Rayburn why he was there, the older man replied, "Maybe Sam Johnson's boy didn't have anyone who cared whether he was sick or not."

For both men, this bond was a natural extension of life back home. As Johnson's father once put it, "People know when you're sick and care when you die."

Another of Johnson's networking tools was the "Little Congress." Congressional aides had formed it in 1919 as a kind of

mock legislature that would give them a chance to master par-
liamentary procedure and public speaking. It had largely
declined into a social club until Johnson used his Dodge Hotel
pals to get himself elected speaker. Under his leadership, weekly
attendance grew from a handful to more than two hundred as
Johnson invited prominent figures such as Huey Long and Fio-
rello La Guardia to speak to the group—invitations that also
served to expand Johnson's circle of contacts. After La Guardia
was elected mayor of New York in 1933, he invited the group to
visit the city, treating them to an outing at the new Radio City
Music Hall.

Another new friend Johnson made in Washington was William White, a young reporter with the Associated Press. "White
was a Texan too," recalls Russell Baker, a former colleague of
White's, "and they became thick from the start and remained so
to the grave." White's duties included covering the Texas congressional delegation. Johnson impressed White with his
shrewdness and his understanding of the people and the issues
on Capitol Hill. White went on to become a prominent war
correspondent during World War II and was hired by the *New
York Times*. He quickly rose to become one of the top reporters
in the *Times*'s Washington bureau, reconnecting with Johnson
while covering the Senate in the 1950s. He became Johnson's
most valuable ally in the press, writing books and articles in the
Times and *Harper's* magazine that featured Johnson as the Senate's master of the art of the possible.

In the early 1930s, Washington was protected from the
harshest impact of the Depression by the cushion of government
salaries. But congressional offices like Kleberg's were flooded
with desperate letters from constituents, and it was Johnson's
job to answer them. And if that wasn't enough, more than
twenty thousand veterans of the First World War descended
upon Washington in 1932 at the conclusion of what was known

as the Bonus March. These veterans had been promised a bonus of one thousand dollars, but it was not payable until 1945. The Depression, however, had made their need for the money immediate, and Congress had given them half in 1931. Now they wanted the rest. They camped out in wooden shacks they threw up on the Anacostia Flats in southeast Washington.

Many in the Hoover administration suspected that the veterans were Bolsheviks, or at least too much influenced by Marxist doctrine. Douglas MacArthur, the army chief of staff, shared this opinion. He was certain that "the Communists hoped to incite revolutionary action." His aide, Major Dwight Eisenhower, felt differently. Most of them, he observed, "were quiet and orderly." When he failed to persuade MacArthur, a frustrated Eisenhower remarked, "I just can't understand how such a damn fool could have gotten to be a general."

Johnson was more successful with his boss. Kleberg had originally opposed the Bonus Bill on the grounds that it would unbalance the budget. But Johnson pointed out that the congressman's mail was running twenty to one in favor of the bill, adding that Kleberg's district contained thousands of veterans who also happened to be voters. In a demonstration of just how influential a congressional aide could be—especially one armed with this kind of persuasive fact—Kleberg changed his mind and became a supporter of the Bonus Bill. It passed the House but failed in the Senate, whereupon a bemedaled MacArthur, astride a white horse, led troops down Pennsylvania Avenue to evict the marchers and burn down their shacks. Johnson never forgot his horror at seeing the marchers being driven down Pennsylvania Avenue "like sheep by a man on a white horse."

The Depression continued to deepen after the Bonus March, with unemployment rising to 25 million and a cascade of bank failures that threatened to overwhelm the nation's financial system. It was in this environment that the nation turned to Franklin Delano Roosevelt, whose decisive victory over President Hoover in the 1932 election promised a New Deal for the American people.

On March 4, 1933, Johnson watched Roosevelt rally his countrymen and declare, "The only thing we have to fear is fear itself." Roosevelt closed the banks for a few days to let the panic subside. Calm was restored and hope began to stir.

Johnson's role as Kleberg's secretary provided him with opportunities to widen his circle of contacts in Texas. Not only did Texans visiting the Washington office find that they could count on the solicitous young aide to take care of them, but Johnson was able to meet many of his fellow Texans when it was necessary for him to travel home on the congressman's behalf. On one of these trips, a major event in his life occurred. During a visit to Austin, a mutual friend introduced him to Claudia Taylor, or Lady Bird, as she was called by her friends and family. He was immediately drawn to this engaging and attractive young woman. It wasn't just her looks and personality, but she had graduated from the University of Texas with all As and Bs and degrees in journalism and history. And it certainly didn't hurt that she was the daughter of a wealthy and prominent East Texas landowner.

Johnson immediately launched an assault that proved irresistible. At their first meeting, he asked her to have breakfast with him the next morning. A few days later, he took her for a drive that ended with a sixty-mile trip so that she could meet his mother. Then he invited her to visit the Klebergs at their mansion on the vast King Ranch. She could not help being impressed. "I felt a little like Alice in Wonderland," she later recalled.

Johnson then invited himself to meet Lady Bird's father, Thomas Taylor. (Her mother had died when she was five.) Taylor liked him, quickly sizing him up as having the right stuff. In a remark that became part of the Johnson legend, he told Lady Bird, "Daughter, you've been bringing home a lot of boys, but this time you've brought a man."

A couple of months later, when Lady Bird was experiencing a moment of doubt about the relationship—not surprisingly, she found Johnson a bit overwhelming—he issued an ultimatum. "Let's get married," he said. "If you say no it just proves that you don't love me enough to dare to marry me. We either do it now or we never will." A week later, they were married.

Lady Bird turned out to be the dream wife for a man of that era. With no career of her own, she was totally supportive of her husband. She saw him as captain of the ship to which she would supply the emotional ballast. Her calm and sensible advice helped keep the ship on a steady course during times of turmoil and trouble. For a personality as volatile as Johnson's, this was essential. As indeed was her forgiving his roving eye without having one of her own.

After a honeymoon in Mexico, Lady Bird and Lyndon returned to Washington, where they rented a small two-room apartment on an unfashionable stretch of Kalorama Road. She plunged into the role of housewife with the aid of a Fannie Farmer cookbook and a knack for budgeting.

Soon, however, their newlywed bliss was disturbed by bad news. Kleberg fired Johnson. The reason may have been that he had grown tired of Johnson's New Dealism or of his tendency to use the office for self-promotion—or both. Another explanation has it that Mrs. Kleberg had turned against Johnson when she discovered a letter suggesting that Johnson had facilitated an affair between the congressman and another woman.

Whatever the reason, Johnson now needed to find a new job.

He turned to his friends and patrons Sam Rayburn and Maury Maverick for help.

Fortuitously, President Roosevelt was launching a new program called the National Youth Administration (NYA). Its purpose was to help young people get educated and find work. A director for the state of Texas had been selected, but Rayburn and Maverick persuaded Roosevelt and his wife, Eleanor, to whom they also appealed, to give the job to their young friend Lyndon Johnson.

Johnson eagerly accepted his new role, seeing it as both a chance to do good and a way to form new friendships and alliances, not just in his congressional district but throughout the state of Texas. On July 25, 1935, he was sworn in. He and Lady Bird moved to Austin, which she said was "like going to heaven." Johnson opened the state NYA headquarters on August 15.

The NYA helped poor young people by putting them to work full-time at thirty dollars per month and part-time at fifteen dollars per month to help them stay in high school or college when they otherwise would be forced to quit by economic necessity. Johnson gave the job his usual total commitment. With just one project—building roadside parks all over Texas—he put thirty-six hundred youths to work by June 1936. In all, he helped more than twenty-eight thousand young Texans. And, unusual for the time, he helped blacks as well as whites.

As was often the case in his long public career, Johnson wasn't just doing good; he was taking care of Lyndon. Not only did the young people in the program become grateful future voters, but the forty-member staff he assembled became the cadre of his future political machine.

Although he was the youngest state director in the program, he did so well that his success won the attention of Franklin and Eleanor Roosevelt. Aubrey Williams, the national head of NYA, was able to look back on his tenure and declare, "Johnson was operating the best NYA program in all of the states."

After Johnson had been at the NYA for less than two years, Buck Buchanan, his district's congressman, died. Although Johnson wasn't even mentioned in an article in the *Austin American-Statesman* about potential successors to Buchanan, he decided to run for the seat.

Here another of Johnson's father-son relationships came into play. Alvin Wirtz, an Austin lawyer and influential Democrat, was twenty years Johnson's senior. But he saw the younger man's promise. He and Johnson decided to make total loyalty to Franklin Roosevelt the centerpiece of the congressional campaign. "Of course there will be those who will be bitter with you," Wirtz told Johnson. "But to hell with them. They're in the minority. People like Roosevelt."

Johnson even embraced Roosevelt's controversial court-packing scheme. And the people agreed. Seven out of eight voters in the district supported the court plan, according to one poll.

Johnson, however, faced a major challenge in getting known throughout the eight-thousand-square-mile district. His home county, Blanco, where Johnson knew practically everyone, was unfortunately the district's smallest. Johnson had to get moving, and so he did—driving to each town in the district, giving more than two hundred speeches, stopping at every filling station to buy a gallon of gas in order to get acquainted with the owner and the other customers, and getting out of his car as he entered each town to walk down the main street shaking hands with everyone he encountered along the way.

This Herculean effort brought victory. Although he got only 28 percent of the vote, that proved enough to give him 3,200 votes more than the closest of his eight opponents.

The campaign may have also provided an early warning of

the moral level on which Johnson's future efforts to win Texas elections would be conducted. It definitely did not err on the high side. Among other sins, Johnson was accused of paying five thousand dollars to President Roosevelt's son Elliott, whose reputation for probity was considerably less than his father's, in exchange for Elliott's endorsement.

When Johnson left Washington to run the NYA in Texas, he had told a friend, "When I come back to Washington, I'm coming back as a congressman." Now, sworn in on May 13, 1937, he was fulfilling that commitment, not as a typical first-termer but as someone who had learned the ropes while serving as Richard Kleberg's secretary.

Furthermore, he was connected in a way that the average first-termer could only dream of. His mentor and friend Sam Rayburn had become House majority leader. Rayburn immediately invited Johnson to join the "board of education," a small group of powerful congressmen who met in Rayburn's hideaway office in the late afternoon to enjoy comradeship and bourbon.

And even before Lyndon returned to the Hill, he had made a more important friend, the president of the United States. He first met and impressed Franklin Roosevelt as director of the Texas NYA. Then, just after Johnson won his seat in Congress, Roosevelt came to Texas and invited him to join the presidential train from Galveston to College Station.

Johnson "came on like a freight train," Roosevelt told a friend, but instead of being offended by the young man's eagerness to impress him, Roosevelt liked him enough to decide to give Johnson a hand when Lyndon arrived in Washington. Roosevelt called his aide Tommy Corcoran and told him, "I've just met the most remarkable young man. I like this boy and you're going to help him with anything you can." Corcoran happened to be the cleverest operator in the Roosevelt entourage, so his backing would prove invaluable in eliminating the bureaucratic roadblocks the young congressman would encounter.

The support of Roosevelt and Rayburn, when combined with Johnson's driving determination, made him one of the most effective first-termers in the history of Capitol Hill. "He got more projects and more money for his district than anybody else," Corcoran later recalled. "He was the best congressman for a district that ever was."

In just his first term, Lyndon got roads paved so that his district's farmers could more easily get their crops to market, he engineered no-collateral loans for poor farm families, and he got dams built that brought public power to a district that had been cruelly handicapped by its lack of electricity. Electricity not only brought light to rural homes, it powered pumps that spared farm wives from the backbreaking chore of carrying water from the well to the house.

It scarcely seemed to matter at the time, but Johnson, by getting the dam and other New Deal projects built, was doing work that advanced the interests of wealthy backers, such as Alvin Wirtz and George and Herman Brown. The Browns owned the powerful construction firm Brown & Root. Unfortunately, Johnson became dependent on the money that poured into his campaign from the Browns' own pockets and their fund-raising from others. This meant that Brown & Root would be a major beneficiary of Johnson programs until the end of his political career, including Vietnam, where the firm was the leading contractor in constructing U.S. bases. Brown & Root would become expert at using "change orders" that permitted the firm to run up costs beyond the bids that had won its contracts, a practice at which it would continue to excel decades later during the Iraq War as the Kellogg, Brown & Root subsidiary of Halliburton.

Another troubling relationship marred Johnson's otherwise triumphant first years in the United States House of Representatives. In 1938, he began an affair with Alice Glass. At a striking six feet, Glass was almost as tall as Johnson. A New York photographer called her "the most beautiful woman I have ever seen." The largely self-educated Glass was as politically sophisticated as Johnson, and, unlike Johnson, she was also sophisticated culturally, with a keen appreciation of music, art, and literature. Indeed, the first extensive contact she had with Johnson occurred when she sought his help securing permanent residence in the States for the young Viennese musician Erich Leinsdorf, an experience that had the incidental effect of kindling Johnson's concern for the plight of European Jews now threatened by the Nazis.

Lyndon began to seek Alice's advice on everything from how to dress to how he could successfully defuse a dispute over a dam with Herman Brown, a backer he could not afford to offend. Awed by Alice's combination of beauty and intelligence, Johnson soon fell in love with her. She, impressed by Johnson's political skill, drawn by his physical magnetism, and perhaps most of all convinced that he shared her idealism, fell just as hard for him.

Unfortunately, two serious problems loomed over the young lovers' idyll. Lyndon was committing adultery, betraying his loyal wife, Lady Bird; and Alice was already the mistress of Charles Marsh, a rich and powerful Texan whose holdings included the *Austin American-Statesman*, a newspaper whose support Lyndon needed.

Alice had been a nineteen-year-old secretary for the Texas legislature when she caught Marsh's eye. Her approach to attracting his affection could not be called conventional. While his wife vacationed on Cape Cod, Marsh had a party at his home in Austin. After he thought the last guest had departed, he decided to sit by the swimming pool to smoke his final cigar of the day. Just then, a naked Glass emerged from the pool with, as Marsh later told a friend, "her long blond hair floating among her fresh young breasts."

Marsh later acquired for Alice a country estate called Long-lea in the Blue Ridge foothills just west of Washington. There they built an influential life together as they entertained the nation's political and cultural elite. If Marsh were to discover the relationship between Alice and Lyndon, the harm to Lyndon's career could be devastating. Johnson's friends wondered why Lyndon would take such a risk. Normally, he made life decisions with considerably more attention to their effect on his career.

But this was no normal situation. Lyndon was so smitten, so deeply in love, that he would sit contentedly for hours listening to Alice read the poetry of Edna St. Vincent Millay. If such behavior seems less than characteristic of Johnson, consider the fact that this man, who was notorious for bragging about his conquests of other women, was never known to boast to anyone of his relationship with Alice. Though both he and Alice were sexually adventurous enough to have other partners, their affair would endure for many years.

Johnson's discretion about his relationship may also have been inspired by a desire to avoid discovery by Charles Marsh. It seems possible that Marsh either did not find out about it or chose to ignore what he knew. If the latter was the case, Marsh may have been motivated by his admiration for Johnson and his desire to be accepted by Johnson as adviser and guide.

According to Marsh's daughter, Marsh did find out about the affair and angrily berated Johnson one evening at Longlea, throwing him out of the house. But after Johnson apologized, the friendship between the two men resumed. "They didn't let her come between them," the daughter said.

Certainly Marsh served as an éminence grise during the next big event in Johnson's career—his campaign for the U.S. Senate in 1941.

3

Trying for the Senate

On April 9, 1941, Senator Morris Sheppard of Texas died of a stroke. Charles Marsh and Alvin Wirtz urged Lyndon Johnson to run for the now vacant seat. Although initial polling showed him supported by just 5 percent of the voters, Johnson's boundless ambition along with the assurance that he would have financing from the deep pockets of George and Herman Brown (the IRS would later determine that the Brown brothers gave three hundred thousand dollars to Johnson's campaign) combined to imbue Johnson with enough confidence to throw his hat into the ring.

Johnson's most dangerous opponent turned out to be W. Lee "Pappy" O'Daniel, who had become a country music star peddling the products of his flour company, using the slogan Pass the Biscuits, Pappy and singing songs such as "The Boy Who Never Gets Too Big to Comb His Mother's Hair." O'Daniel had propelled himself to the Texas governorship in 1938, and he, too, had now set his sights on Sheppard's Senate seat.

Johnson campaigned under the slogan Roosevelt and Unity, emphasizing the need for the nation to come together under Franklin Roosevelt's leadership to confront the looming threat from Nazi Germany. A grateful Roosevelt tried to help Johnson. "I can't take part in a Texas primary [but] if you ask me about Lyndon himself," he told reporters, "I can only tell you what is perfectly true—you all know he is a very old and close friend of mine." Roosevelt's cabinet pitched in as well, enabling Johnson to announce one new federal project in Texas after another. The Johnson campaign reflected both the liberal idealism of Marsh and the practical political genius of twenty-four-year-old John Connally, who ran the nuts-and-bolts side. The combination of their strategy and Johnson's tirelessness on the stump produced an amazing climb in the polls, culminating in an election eve lead for Johnson of 4.5 percentage points over O'Daniel.

On the morning after the election, when 96 percent of the votes had been counted, Johnson led by a margin of 5,000 votes. Johnson and Connally, eager to proclaim victory, had encouraged their county leaders to report results to the state election commission in Austin as quickly as possible. This was a big mistake. Johnson's opponents now knew exactly how many votes they had to get from the remaining 4 percent. It just so happened that they controlled enough of the counties that had not reported their vote and of the counties whose early already-reported votes they could change that they were able to make O'Daniel the winner.

Johnson took the defeat well. He knew he had made a truly incredible comeback from the first poll and that he had really won. He was confident he would win next time, having learned a great secret—to be sure that he had enough votes in reserve to make up any deficit in the first count.

Now Johnson returned to Washington to make one of the most important votes of his career—the Selective Training and Service Act of 1940 was up for renewal in August 1941. Johnson felt so strongly that the draft should be extended that he made only his second speech on the floor of the House since his arrival in Congress four years before. The first draftees were threatening to go "over the hill in October"—that is, they would be leaving the army after the expiration of one year of service, for which they had originally been drafted.

Isolationists in Congress had been emboldened by recent developments in Europe: Britain's survival of the blitz and the German invasion of the Soviet Union on June 22, 1941. They now argued that the United States no longer had to worry about saving Britain and that the Communists and the Nazis would neutralize each other. So the vote on the draft extension was going to be close. In the event, it proved to be as close as possible— passing the House of Representatives by one vote. Now Lyndon Johnson, along with all the other supporters of the bill, could legitimately claim that his was that one vote, for in truth each vote was crucial.

How crucial became clear with Japan's attack on Pearl Harbor on December 7 and Adolf Hitler's declaration of war against the United States four days later. The U.S. Army, before the draft, had consisted of 275,000 men. With the extended draft, the army now had 1.6 million soldiers in uniform at the time Pearl Harbor was bombed.

The lesson Lyndon Johnson and many other Americans took from Pearl Harbor was that the isolationists and appeasers—all those who kept their heads embedded in the sand while Germany and Japan threatened world peace in the 1930s—had been dead wrong.

The war confronted Johnson with the challenge to fulfill a campaign pledge he had made—to join any draftees sent to fight abroad. By December the thirty-three-year-old congressman had wangled a lieutenant commander's commission in the U.S. Naval Reserve. This meant that if he were to go to war he was likely to do so in a more comfortable role than that enjoyed by the typical draftee. Still, Johnson was sticking by his campaign promise. On December 8, he sent a telegram to President Roosevelt: "As a member of the Naval Reserve of the United States Navy, I hereby urgently request my commander in chief to assign me immediately to active duty with the fleet."

Since Johnson had no training to equip him to perform any duty on a warship, he must have known that his request was unlikely to be granted. Instead, the navy assigned him to a desk job. He retained his role in the House by arranging a "leave of absence." Lady Bird and Nellie Connally—the wife of John Connally, Johnson's top aide, who had also gone into the navy—ran the congressional office.

The navy made Johnson responsible for expediting war production in Texas and on the West Coast. He threw himself into the assignment with characteristic enthusiasm and determination. "It is time to quit 'conferring' and go to work," he told the bureaucrats responsible for production bottlenecks. "The road to hell is paved with indecision and inaction."

Johnson's inspection trips to the West Coast were not entirely dedicated to the war effort. His agenda also included parties, women, and visits to Hollywood studios where he met Cecil B. DeMille and other film luminaries and learned from photographers the poses that showed the best side of his face.

On the whole, however, Johnson performed effectively in his production job. Still, he realized that service overseas was necessary if he was to honor his campaign pledge completely. President Roosevelt understood and assigned him to visit General Douglas MacArthur, newly arrived in Australia to take command of American forces being assembled there to stop the Japanese onslaught, which by April had overrun the Dutch East Indies, all of the Philippines except for the tiny island fortress of Corregidor, and all of Malaya, including the supposedly impregnable British base at Singapore. On May 1, 1942, Johnson left for Pearl Harbor and flew from there to New Zealand and Australia.

At first, MacArthur feared Johnson, seeing him as a spy for the president, which, of course, Johnson was, but Johnson was also sincere in wanting to understand MacArthur's needs so that he could communicate them to Washington. Johnson's skill in massaging the general's not inconsiderable ego soon had MacArthur promising to let him see firsthand what those needs were.

In the course of his fact-gathering, Johnson actually flew on one combat mission, a bombing run against a base the Japanese had seized at Lae on the north coast of New Guinea. Johnson's plane—a B-26 two-engine bomber christened the Heckling Hare by its crew—was attacked, first by one Japanese Zero fighter, and then by a squadron of seven. The Zeros, much faster and more maneuverable aircraft than the B-26, quickly riddled the Heckling Hare with bullets and small cannon fire. Amazingly, the plane managed to escape, even shooting down one of the Zeros.

Although Johnson had not fired a shot, he had behaved admirably during the fight—"cool as a cucumber" and "just as calm as if we were on a sightseeing tour," said two crew members. MacArthur awarded him the Silver Star, the second-highest decoration for courage under fire. The only problem was that no other member of the Heckling Hare crew received any award, even though they had participated more actively in the battle than Johnson.

Johnson filed a frank report about the shortage of supplies and the inadequacies of the existing equipment. But by now he had had enough of military life. His demeanor aboard the Heckling Hare had been a triumph for a man described by a classmate at San Marcos as "an absolute physical coward," but he did not want to endure such a challenge again.

And so he was relieved when President Roosevelt asked all members of Congress serving in the armed forces to return to their seats in the House or Senate. Four congressmen decided to surrender their seats and remain in the fight. Johnson was one of four others who chose to follow their commander in chief's wishes.

The capital to which Johnson had returned was now almost completely preoccupied with the war. As Roosevelt himself put it in describing his role, Dr. New Deal had been replaced by Dr. Win the War.

The war news, which had been all bad through March, had turned better, at least for a while, in the spring of 1942. An air raid on Tokyo had been carried out in April by U.S. Army Air Force bombers daringly brought within range of Japan by a navy carrier and improbably launched from its short deck even though they had been designed to take off from much longer runways on land. In May at the Battle of the Coral Sea, a carrier group commanded by Admiral Frank Jack Fletcher turned back a Japanese invasion force headed for Port Moresby on the south coast of New Guinea, from which Japanese bombers could have raided Australia. And at the Battle of Midway in early June, Admiral Fletcher and Admiral Raymond Spruance won a great victory over the Japanese main fleet, sinking four aircraft carriers. Then, in early August, America launched its first major counterattack on the Japanese by invading the island of Guadalcanal.

But there the good news seemed to end. In North Africa, the German general Erwin Rommel seemed unstoppable as he threatened Alexandria and the Suez Canal itself. In Russia, German troops had reached the Caucasus and Stalingrad. And at Guadalcanal, the Japanese were putting up a fierce fight, both on the ground and at sea, even threatening to dislodge the American beachhead.

Gloom settled on Washington and the country at large. Criticism of Roosevelt, muted in the first months of the war, now grew louder. The United States and Great Britain, with

Roosevelt yielding to Prime Minister Winston Churchill's wishes to postpone a cross-channel attack on Europe, had agreed on an Allied landing in French North Africa, and scheduled it to begin on October 30, 1942.

Roosevelt saw the political peril in the bad war news. He wanted the invasion to happen before the congressional elections scheduled for November 3. "Please," he begged General George Marshall, "make it before election day."

Lyndon Johnson was again charged with running the Democratic congressional campaign, but his magic could not reverse the anti-Roosevelt tide. The North African invasion, delayed until November 8, came too late. The result was a severe Democratic defeat. The party lost forty-four seats in the House, and its majority was now down to thirteen, the smallest in Franklin Roosevelt's presidency.

The country seemed to be taking a conservative turn, one that had begun in the 1938 midterm elections, when Democratic margins in the House and Senate were sharply reduced. This trend had been interrupted in 1940 by the voters' faith in Roosevelt's international leadership, which enabled the president to win a third term and carry the Democrats to triumph in Congress as well. Now that faith had been damaged by the war news, enabling the conservatives to stage a revival.

Certainly, the conservative tide was strong in Texas, forcing Johnson to tone down his pro-Roosevelt rhetoric on visits back home. Still, he remained loyal to the president in Washington and easily won another term in the House in the November election.

In his home life, there was more bad news for Lyndon Johnson. Lady Bird's patience with Johnson's philandering was strained by evidence that it continued unabated. A film Johnson had taken of his trip to Australia included a brief shot of a very attractive young woman whose presence Lyndon refused to explain when his wife asked, "Who's that?" In his diary of the trip, he refers to calls to "Tess" and cables to "Miss Jesus." Since Lady Bird complained that she had not heard from Lyndon, she does not appear to have been the recipient. In addition, Lady Bird suffered a second miscarriage in 1942 and had to fight with Lyndon over the purchase of a house even though it was her money that would pay for it. Finally she exploded: "I want that house. Every woman wants a home of her own. I've lived out of a suitcase ever since we've been married. I have no home to look forward to. I have no children to look forward to. I have nothing to look forward to but another election."

Johnson sought out his aide John Connally for advice. "What should I do?" he asked.

Connally answered, "I'd buy the house," which is exactly what Johnson proceeded to do.

Johnson also sought to placate Lady Bird by arranging the purchase of an Austin radio station, KTBC, for her to run. KTBC and its sister television station that the Johnsons created a few years later were to benefit over the years from one favorable Federal Communications Commission (FCC) ruling after another— rulings that made the Johnsons rich. At one time, the television station was permitted to fill its schedule with whatever programs it wanted to select from the three major networks, a privilege not granted to any other station.

Johnson claimed that he never intervened with the FCC on behalf of his family's radio and television holdings. But his well-known influence with President Roosevelt and subsequently his powerful positions in the House and Senate made this claim seem disingenuous to many observers.

Especially in KTBC's early days, Johnson meddled in its management, sometimes playing the dominant role, so it's hard to believe that the station was completely successful in placating Lady Bird as he had intended. More important to the restoration of her happiness in the marriage may have been the birth of her first child, Lynda, in 1944—another daughter, Luci, came along in 1947—which meant that she now had not only the home she had longed for but a family to fill it.

Meanwhile, Johnson's continued support of Roosevelt in Washington manifested itself most clearly when the president vetoed a tax bill in 1943 as "not for the needy but for the greedy." Fewer than one out of four congressmen voted to sustain the president's veto. Lyndon Johnson was one of them.

In the 1944 election, both Johnson and his mentor Sam Rayburn, who had become Speaker of the House in 1940, came under attack from Texas conservatives for their support of Roosevelt. But the war news was good that year. The Allies took Rome, landed in Normandy, and by election day in November appeared to have routed Hitler's army, which was hastily retreating to Germany itself.

Johnson and Rayburn were reelected by wide margins, and Roosevelt defeated Governor Thomas E. Dewey of New York to win his fourth term. The Democrats also increased their congressional majorities. But on April 12, 1945, as Allied armies were sweeping to victory in Europe, Franklin Roosevelt suffered a stroke as he sat on the porch of his tiny cottage in Warm Springs, Georgia, and died two hours later.

For many Americans, faith in Roosevelt had become the bedrock of their lives. Deprived of solid ground by his death, their beliefs wavered. Some, like former vice president Henry Wallace, became more liberal. Others, including Lyndon Johnson, moved to the right. The new president, Harry Truman, though now remembered affectionately by historians, did not strike his contemporaries as an inspiring leader. He supported a continuation of the New Deal in his speeches and policy proposals, but his appointments tended to be conservative.

Johnson's and Truman's move to the right was tiny compared

to the giant shift taking place in the country as a whole. The 1946 congressional election became a total triumph for the Republican Party, which won control of both the House and the Senate. Sam Rayburn was out as Speaker of the House, replaced by Joseph Martin of Massachusetts. And in the Senate, the new majority leader was Robert A. Taft, whose conservatism would earn him the title of Mr. Republican.

A series of strikes had occurred after the war, as labor unions sought the pay increases that wartime wage controls had denied their members and as a postwar inflation began to erode real incomes. The United Auto Workers had asked General Motors for a wage increase of thirty-eight cents an hour, or from $44.80 to $58 for a forty-hour week for the average worker. When GM countered with a proposal of only ten cents an hour, the union went on strike.

The strike lasted 113 days and was finally settled with a seemingly modest raise of eighteen cents an hour. But for a public hungry for new cars, after none had been produced during the war, the delay was maddening, and the unions were blamed. Other strikes proved costly for their communities. In Pittsburgh, a strike by thirty-five hundred electrical workers put one hundred thousand more workers out of a job, further inflaming antiunion sentiment.

The result was the antiunion Taft-Hartley Act, passed by the new Republican Congress over President Truman's veto in 1947. Although far from being the "slave-labor" law that some union leaders called it, the act's main purpose was to limit the unions' ability to organize workers and to maintain their membership. Still, Lyndon Johnson voted for it, declaring that he was determined to control the "irresponsible, racketeering, self-inflated labor leaders." And, in what must have been an attempt to appease his segregationist constituents, he voted to kill the Fair Employment Practices Commission (FEPC), which President

Roosevelt had established to provide equal employment rights for African Americans.

Johnson continued his support of a strong national defense, urging a reinstitution of the draft, which had been allowed to lapse after the war. He also campaigned for a seventy-group air force, which would have the incidental effect of aiding Texas with its many air force bases and aircraft plants. In foreign affairs he gave strong support to the Truman Doctrine, designed to prevent Greece and Turkey from being taken over by the Communists, and for the Marshall Plan, to promote the economic recovery of Europe.

The legitimate fear of Communist encroachment in Europe unfortunately tended to encourage an unreasonable fear of Communists here at home. The House Un-American Activities Committee engaged in witch hunts, and President Truman ordered a loyalty board for government agencies to screen civil servants for pro-Communist leanings. Under Truman's order, government employees did not have the right to confront their accusers.

Some real Communists were turned up by both the House and the loyalty program, but far too many innocents lost their jobs and had their reputations tarnished. Johnson was largely silent about these abuses. He was changing his reputation from all-out liberal to moderate conservative.

Meanwhile, Harry Truman had managed to alienate both northern liberals and southern conservatives. In 1948, former vice president Henry Wallace led the Democrats' far-left faction into a new party, and Governor Strom Thurmond of South Carolina did the same for the party's more rabid segregationists. Truman's standing in the polls, high in the early months of his presidency, had sunk almost out of sight, and remained there as 1948 began. His conservative tendencies had disturbed liberals while his advocacy of the FEPC, antilynching, and anti–poll tax legislation along with his desegregation of the armed forces

frightened many in the South. Most Americans, however, supported his foreign policy. After the Soviet-backed coup in
Czechoslovakia in February 1948, only a small minority, including Wallace's Progressive Party, remained unconvinced of the
danger of Stalinism. But even the support Truman enjoyed for
his foreign policy could not rescue him from another factor in
his unpopularity: embarrassment at his down-to-earth style
that did not fit the national image of what a president should be.

Democratic prospects as the 1948 election approached
seemed gloomy. The Republicans were so confident of winning
that they felt safe in giving the nomination to Tom Dewey, who
had already lost one presidential election and who even one of
his most loyal supporters described as "cold, cold as a February
iceberg."

Despite the Democrats' poor prospects, Lyndon Johnson
decided to make another run for the U.S. Senate. Texas seemed
likely to remain safely in the Democratic column in the general
election, but the Democratic primary posed a difficult challenge because of the trend toward the right among Texans. The
principal candidate opposing Johnson for the nomination would
be the state's very conservative and very popular governor Coke
Stevenson.

Johnson had reasons to dislike and fear Stevenson. Stevenson
forces had helped Pappy O'Daniel defeat Johnson in 1941 because
they wanted to see Stevenson, who was then lieutenant governor,
get the top job in Austin. Stevenson was also a racist, an isolation-
ist, and much more consistently conservative than Johnson.

Still, he was a formidable opponent, having twice won reelection for governor by wide margins. He was seen as a skilled
administrator who had balanced the state's budget. In the July
24 primary, Stevenson actually defeated Johnson, 477,000 votes
to 405,000 votes. Fortunately for Johnson, there was a third
candidate in the race, George Peddy, who managed to attract

support from 337,000 voters. No candidate having received a majority, there now had to be a runoff. Johnson faced a daunting challenge; he needed to attract at least two-thirds of Peddy's supporters to win. To Lady Bird, the situation "looked hopeless."

Johnson responded by redoubling his already strenuous campaigning, making so many speeches that by election eve his voice croaked. Stevenson helped by making a fool of himself. On a visit to Washington, he was interviewed by Jack Anderson, the young assistant to the powerful columnist Drew Pearson. When asked for his position on the Taft-Hartley Act, Stevenson replied, "You get me off up here away from my notes." Pearson, who was one of the well-placed "connections" Johnson had made during his early days in Washington, then attacked Stevenson, saying he had "evaded more issues and dodged more questions than any recent performer in a city noted for question-dodging." Pearson's column ran in newspapers throughout Texas.

On election night, August 28, the race proved too close to call. In the days thereafter, the lead seesawed back and forth. On September 2, the Texas election bureau announced its final unofficial result, with Stevenson the winner by 362 votes.

The key word was "unofficial," and here the Johnson forces showed they had learned the lessons of their defeat in 1941. They had held back final official returns from the counties where they controlled the election machinery. As these counties began to report their official returns, an astonishing number of new votes for Johnson were discovered by the county election officials. Duval County found 425. In just one precinct in Jim Wells County, 203 new Johnson votes appeared. They increased the total votes for the Senate in that precinct to 1,028, though the precinct had been given only six hundred ballots, which aroused suspicion as to the sanctity of the electoral process. Nonetheless, the Texas election bureau proclaimed Johnson the winner by 162 votes.

Stevenson appealed to the State Democratic Executive Committee. A long, sweaty, and acrimonious meeting on September 14 yielded a ruling that Johnson had won by 87 votes.

Stevenson went to court, securing an injunction from a federal judge that kept Johnson's name off the general-election ballot, pending an investigation of possible fraud in Jim Wells County. Johnson couldn't wait for an investigation—he not only had reason to fear the result, but he knew that the ballots had to be printed in order to get to polling places in time for the November election. But Johnson's Texas lawyers found themselves unable to agree on what to do next. "Where's Abe?" Johnson asked.

A call to Abe Fortas in Washington produced the knight in shining armor Johnson desperately needed. Fortas, a friend that Johnson had made while serving in the House, proved his genius—he had been called "the most brilliant legal mind to ever come out of Yale Law School"—by devising a strategy that quickly got the appeal of the injunction to the United States Supreme Court. There, Fortas knew that the justice responsible for overseeing the federal judge was the liberal Hugo Black, more likely to be sympathetic to Johnson than to the very conservative Stevenson. Furthermore, in the early 1940s, Johnson and Fortas had been entertained at Black's home in Alexandria, Virginia. If that wasn't enough, Johnson had the support of other Washington friends. Joseph Rauh, who assisted Fortas in the case, later said he believed that still another of Johnson's Washington connections, Tommy Corcoran, had quietly spoken to Black on Johnson's behalf. Although such intervention was considered improper, Corcoran was enough of an operator to make the suspicion plausible. And others, including Attorney General Tom Clark, Sam Rayburn, and even Harry Truman himself, were also rumored to have spoken to Black on Johnson's behalf.

And even without the influence of friends, the merits of the law favored Johnson. The Supreme Court had traditionally let states decide election disputes within their borders, a doctrine that was to prevail until *Bush v. Gore*. In 1948, Black continued the tradition, overruling the federal judge and letting the decision of the Texas State Democratic Executive Committee stand.

In the general election, Johnson won by an impressive majority, actually a little bit better than two to one, as he won more than 702,000 votes. Harry Truman, helped by his own tireless whistle-stop campaigning, by the contrast between his warm humanity and Dewey's coldness, and by the success of the Berlin airlift, which dominated the news during the fall, did even better than Johnson, carrying Texas with 750,000 votes. He also won enough other states to be reelected president, climaxing one of the great comebacks in American electoral history.

4

The Art of the Possible

The word "subdued" would rarely rank among the most apt to describe Lyndon Johnson, but for a time after his election to the United States Senate in 1948 it fit. His victory by an 87-vote margin had not been a resounding vote of confidence from his constituents. Furthermore, the opponent who had almost defeated him—and indeed had won in the eyes of many observers, who were convinced that Johnson had stolen the election—was a conservative whose strong showing signaled the waning influence of the New Deal in Texas. And the walkout of the Dixiecrats from the 1948 Democratic National Convention, coupled with Strom Thurmond's victory in four southern states in the general election, provided even more dramatic evidence of a tilt to the right in the politics of the South.

Finally, if one saw Harry Truman's victory in the 1948 election as more the triumph of a likable human being over the cold fish Tom Dewey than evidence of a liberal resurgence, one could conclude that the national conservative trend continued, a conclusion quickly reinforced by the death of most liberal initiatives in the Congress that convened in January 1949.

A little-noticed reason for postwar conservatism came in the attitude of returning veterans. Having survived the Depression and the war, they had had enough risk and drama in their lives. Now they wanted life to be nice, normal, and regular—as in the Andy Hardy movies. An attempt was made to organize the returning soldiers and sailors into the American Veterans Committee to fight for liberal objectives. But most veterans wanted no part of it. It was not a matter of subscribing to right-wing ideology. Friedrich Hayek and Ayn Rand didn't reach any more of them than did the liberal American Veterans Committee. They simply no longer wanted to be warriors for any cause. They wanted the safe family life with the picket fence portrayed in new versions of the Hardy family like the popular radio (and later television) show *Father Knows Best*. That is why so many of them chose to work for large organizations that offered job security. They sought stability to keep things the same, which more than anything explains the tremendous majorities soon to be racked up by the father who knew best, Dwight Eisenhower.

During 1948 and 1949, the country was dismayed to learn that atomic secrets had been given to the Russians with indications that American spies had been involved and that Alger Hiss, a former New Deal official, was accused of being a Soviet spy, with evidence persuasive enough to trouble even loyal Democrats.

It was with all these signs that he should moderate his positions—if not abandon the New Deal and move to the right—that Johnson's first year in the Senate got under way. A further reason for him to be subdued came from the culture of his new legislative home. The United States Senate did not welcome the brash. Deference was expected of junior members. Johnson received a quick lesson in Senate culture when he attempted to pressure the Senate president pro tem, Carl Hayden, for a large suite of offices, only to have his importunings ignored.

Johnson got the point. If brashness wouldn't work, he would try humility. He soon verged on becoming Uriah Heep as he fawned on his seniors.

The one he fawned on the most was Richard Russell of Georgia. Russell was a senior member of the Armed Services Committee and the most powerful Democratic senator. And like Sam Rayburn, he was a lonely bachelor. In other words, he was an ideal target for Lyndon and Lady Bird. So it didn't take long for Russell to be won over and for Johnson to refer to him as one of his daddies.

Among the men Johnson would say were just like a daddy to him, it appears he really meant it about four—Alvin Wirtz, Sam Rayburn, Franklin Roosevelt, and Richard Russell.

Johnson also sought the help of a younger man. Bobby Baker was a Senate aide still in his early twenties, but he had already acquired the reputation of knowing more about the Senate than anyone else, especially about how to persuade senators based on his understanding of their political and personal—including sexual—needs, and sometimes even their convictions. Baker found Johnson to be his most avid pupil. The two formed an alliance that would endure for fourteen years.

Following Baker's advice, and proceeding in the firm belief that there could be no such thing as too much sucking up, Johnson began to win the favor of his seniors. Eventually, he was even rewarded with an extra office by Carl Hayden.

Another subduing factor for Johnson, this in his personal life, came in the late summer of 1949, with the suspension of his affair with Helen Gahagan Douglas, who had succeeded Alice Glass as his number-one mistress four years earlier. Douglas, a stage and screen actress and the wife of the actor Melvyn Douglas, had been elected to Congress from California in 1944. She and Johnson found themselves falling in love as they mourned the death in April 1945 of Franklin Roosevelt, the president they both worshipped. It was not surprising Johnson was attracted to Douglas. She was another Alice Glass, combining sex appeal with a passion for politics. Their affair became so well known on the Hill that it seems likely that Johnson wanted to show her off because she was so beautiful and accomplished. The affair continued on an occasional basis for many years but ended as a major involvement for both parties when Douglas decided to run for the Senate and left Washington to begin her campaign. She would ultimately lose to Richard Nixon in November 1950. Nixon won in another indication of the tenor of the times by painting Douglas as soft on Communism and calling her the "Pink Lady."

Johnson's new conservatism soon found expression. He demonstrated his allegiance to the South by agreeing to vote with its senators against cloture, which would have shut off debate and permitted Truman's civil rights legislation to come to a vote. On the protection of oil and gas interests, he sided with conservatives, and incidentally displayed his dedication to the business that had become the mainstay of the Texas economy.

In perhaps his most controversial concession to the conservatives, Johnson led the fight against a leading public-power advocate, Leland Olds, to be confirmed for a new term as a member of the Federal Power Commission. Although there was absolutely no evidence that Olds was a Communist in 1949, some of his writings in the 1920s and early 1930s had seemed sympathetic to Russia. Johnson asked the Senate, "Shall we have a commissioner or a commissar?" Olds was already enough of a hero to the liberal wing of the Democratic Party that this one action made many of its members perennially suspicious of Johnson's motives. And, even more costly to Johnson, it lost him the support of Drew Pearson, the influential columnist whose early praise had been a significant factor in Johnson's rise to power.

Those senators who had not gotten the message about the country's tilt to the right received a convincing lesson in the 1950 midterm election. Their teacher was the junior senator from Wisconsin, Joseph McCarthy, who in January of that year broke out of the pack of relatively obscure backbenchers to make his infamous speech in Wheeling, West Virginia, accusing the State Department of being chockablock with Communists. He claimed to have a list of their names, but he would never provide it.

The impact of his charges on the public was heightened by a jury's finding that same month that Alger Hiss was guilty of perjury in denying that he gave State Department documents to a former Communist agent, Whittaker Chambers, and by the cases against Klaus Fuchs, Harry Gold, and Julius and Ethel Rosenberg, all of whom were accused of involvement in passing atomic secrets to the Soviet Union.

The North Korean Communists topped it all off with their invasion of South Korea in late June 1950, which triggered the subsequent deployment of American and United Nations troops to defend South Korea. In the fall congressional elections, several Democratic senators who had been targets of Joe McCarthy went down to defeat. They included Millard Tydings of Maryland, Francis Myers of Pennsylvania, who was the Democratic whip, and Scott Lucas of Illinois, the Democratic majority leader. A substantial Democratic majority in the Senate was reduced to two.

Senator Ernest McFarland of Arizona was elected majority leader, and with the help of Richard Russell and the oil and gas millionaire Senator Robert Kerr of Oklahoma, Johnson was elected majority whip. The whip's main responsibility involved rounding up votes and knowing where each senator stood when a bill reached the floor. With Bobby Baker's aid, Johnson performed the role superbly.

In 1951, Harry Truman fired General Douglas MacArthur for insubordination after MacArthur made public a letter he had sent to House Republican leader Joseph Martin strongly disagreeing with Truman's policy. For one thing, MacArthur wanted to retake North Korea, but most of Washington's policy makers disagreed. They, including Harry Truman, had supported MacArthur's decision the previous fall to cross the thirty-eighth parallel to invade the North after his spectacular landing at Inchon had turned the tide of the war. But they decided that the invasion had been a mistake after it led to the Chinese Communist intervention and a disastrous retreat by U.S. forces. The influential columnist Walter Lippmann argued that the U.S. policy of containing Communism should not involve aggression of its own. If the Communists acted aggressively as they had done in the case of the Berlin blockade in 1948–49, U.S. policy should be to restore the status quo ante, to restore the situation as it was before the blockade, as with the Berlin airlift. Similarly in Korea, the United States should have pushed the Communists out of South Korea but not invaded the North.

MacArthur had even more alarming proposals, including the use of atomic weapons against the Chinese. All of this disturbed Johnson and other senators, as did his insubordination against Truman, which they regarded as violating the American tradition of civilian control of the military.

The general returned to the United States to enormous crowds, who seemed to regard him as a conquering hero even though he had been caught with his pants down by the intervention of the Chinese Communists in Korea the previous November.

Johnson, however, remained loyal to Truman and the principle of civilian control of the military. In a Senate hearing, he questioned MacArthur in a solicitous manner that nonetheless glaringly revealed the general's ignorance of world affairs. Bobby Baker called it "the biggest honeyfucking I have ever seen in my life." Johnson's loyalty to Truman in the MacArthur case cost him little in the regard of his southern colleagues. Many of them, especially Richard Russell, felt a profound distaste for the general's grandstanding.

But Johnson had his own hawkish side. In one speech, he even urged immediate retaliation against the Soviet Union in the event of Communist aggression anywhere. Nonetheless, despite his bellicose rhetoric on the one "fight or don't fight" policy decision in which he participated during the 1950s, Johnson proved a reluctant warrior. In 1954, when the French were close to losing their colony in Indochina to insurgents, they asked for the U.S. Air Force to come to their rescue. Secretary of State John Foster Dulles, who favored granting the request, asked Johnson and Richard Russell to gauge the Senate's reaction. They effectively squelched the proposal by reporting back that at least forty Democratic senators would oppose intervention.

In 1952, Johnson had to make a choice that risked at least some of his southern support, especially from his fellow Texas Democrats. The Republican presidential nominee, Dwight Eisenhower, enjoyed great popularity in the Lone Star State, popularity not shared by the Democratic nominee, Governor Adlai Stevenson of Illinois. The result: Eisenhower won the support of a large number of Texas Democrats, led by the current governor, Allan Shivers, and former governor Coke Stevenson, the man who had come within a whisker of defeating Johnson in the 1948 Senate race.

Under the urging of the widow of his idol, Eleanor Roosevelt, and other northern liberals, Johnson decided to support Adlai Stevenson. This meant that even though Eisenhower overwhelmed Stevenson at the polls, and his coattails carried a majority of Republicans to power in both houses of Congress,

Johnson emerged with enough support from both the liberal and conservative wings of the Democratic Party to be elected minority leader to replace Ernest McFarland, who had lost reelection in Arizona to an up-and-comer named Barry Goldwater.

As minority leader, Johnson emphasized cooperation with the Eisenhower White House. He and his old friend Sam Rayburn, the former Speaker and now House minority leader, were often photographed emerging from meetings with the president. Eisenhower represented the moderate wing of the Republican Party, having defeated the conservative Robert Taft for his party's nomination, and on many issues he and Johnson and Rayburn were not that far apart. This was particularly true in the area of foreign policy, where the bipartisan tradition established by the Republican senator Arthur Vandenberg and the Truman administration in 1946 (that "politics stops at the water's edge") continued to prevail. Eisenhower, with Democratic support, ended the Korean War or, to be more precise, obtained a lasting truce in 1953 that left the two sides roughly divided by the original boundary at the thirty-eighth parallel.

In the 1954 congressional elections, the voters' customary off-year preference for the out-of-power party gave the Democrats control of the House and Senate. Johnson became the majority leader, and Rayburn returned to the Speaker's chair.

Johnson had proved an outstanding whip. Now he was to become an even better majority leader. His long legislative career had enabled him to hone his skill at leaning on his colleagues—something he literally seemed to do in an iconic photograph in which he looms over the diminutive Senator Theodore Green of Rhode Island—in order to bend them to his will. He knew what motivational buttons to push, as well as those to avoid, with each senator.

Once again Baker, whom Johnson had made secretary of the

Senate, proved invaluable, as did the excellent staff Johnson had assembled with the help of John Connally, who had briefly returned to Washington in 1949 to put together Johnson's Senate office. The tireless Walter Jenkins, Horace Busby, Harry McPherson, and George Reedy were notable for their intelligence and their loyalty to Johnson, which would continue into the White House.

In his first year as majority leader, Johnson took on Senator Joseph McCarthy, who had proved a thorn in the side of the Democrats and of Dwight Eisenhower. Most senators shared Johnson's dislike of McCarthy, but they also feared him, and that fear had kept them from acting against him until 1955. Opportunity then presented itself during hearings about McCarthy's accusation that the army had promoted a Communist dentist. McCarthy revealed enough of his true self to cause his opposing counsel, Joseph Welch, to ask, "Have you no sense of decency, sir? At long last, have you left no sense of decency?" The public saw that McCarthy was a bully and a blowhard, enabling Johnson to mobilize senators who had heretofore trembled at McCarthy's threats to rise up and vote to censure him. McCarthy was finished. And for a while at least, so was the extreme right wing of the Republican Party.

Johnson's success in the Senate had him beginning to consider a run for the presidency in 1956. But that thought was short-lived. His success had come at a cost. His heavy work schedule had put him under enormous strain. On July 2, 1955, he had a heart attack.

He had been drinking and smoking far too much. Enough for his mentor Sam Rayburn to confront him with the need to cut down. Bobby Baker estimated that Johnson downed a fifth of scotch every day, and he was a chain smoker.

Another factor in the strain on Johnson was the difficulty of keeping the liberal and conservative wings of his party happy.

He needed support from both, not only to maintain his power as majority leader but also to be in a position to run for president. At a press conference on the afternoon of July 2, when asked why he didn't support a liberal immigration reform, he exploded, berating the reporter and canceling the press conference.

Later that afternoon, he was driven across the Potomac to the Virginia hunt country estate of his friend and backer George Brown of Brown & Root. On the way, Johnson began to experience discomfort. After his arrival, Brown noticed that Johnson was sweating profusely. Brown suspected heart trouble and asked another guest, Senator Clinton Anderson, who had recently recovered from a heart attack, to take a look at Johnson.

Anderson immediately said, "My God, man! You're having a heart attack!" At first, Johnson resisted calling a doctor, fearing that news of a heart attack would kill his presidential prospects. But that fear was quickly replaced by the fear of death as the pain grew more severe. A doctor came and ordered Johnson taken to the navy hospital in Bethesda, Maryland. When he got there, the first thing he asked his doctor was if he would be able to smoke again.

When the doctor said no, Johnson sighed, "I'd rather have my pecker cut off."

The heart attack proved serious enough for his doctors to worry about his chances for survival, which they put at fifty-fifty. The first four days were touch and go. But with Lady Bird faithfully at his side, day and night—she literally did not leave the hospital for a week—he began to feel better and the danger of death receded.

The *Congressional Record* was filled with speeches expressing the warm regard of Johnson's colleagues from the Senate and House. As soon as he was able to receive visitors, they began to line up outside his hospital room. President Eisen-

hower came, as did Vice President Richard Nixon and congressional leaders, including Sam Rayburn. Bobby Baker had spent
Johnson's first few days in the hospital sitting faithfully in the
waiting room until Johnson was finally able to see him.

After he was released from the hospital and spent a few
weeks at his Washington home, Johnson was flown to his ranch
in Texas by the Pedernales River. There he remained until late in
the year. In a couple of respects, he proved to be an ideal
patient. He gave up cigarettes completely. When asked if he
missed smoking, he replied, "Every minute of every day." He
also became a dedicated dieter, cutting down to fifteen hundred
calories a day. Cantaloupe became his favorite food. And he lost
an incredible 50 pounds, reducing his weight to a trim 170.

His diet may have been good, but his mood was not. He was
depressed. Johnson feared that his chances of becoming president had been reduced to zero. His depression would come and
go for the next few months, but it dominated his mind most of
the time.

Relief came in the form of four thousand letters from well-
wishers and from numerous laudatory editorials in the nation's
newspapers. Lady Bird and his staff read each one to him. He
insisted that all the letters be answered and the editorial writers
thanked. And between the staff and Lady Bird, the job got done.

But as the depression lifted, his behavior began to depart
from the "good patient" standard.

A lovely young woman from Austin arrived to serve as one of
Johnson's secretaries. A petite contrast to the statuesque Alice
Glass and Helen Gahagan Douglas, she nevertheless proved
equally irresistible to Johnson. And though Johnson had many
affairs with his secretaries during his long career, this one was
special. Soon he began slipping into her room at night, which
required him to climb the stairs against his doctor's orders.

On at least one evening, Lady Bird became aware that

Johnson had gone upstairs. The secretary was sufficiently attractive that it is difficult to believe Lady Bird did not suspect "something" was going on. In any event, the "something" continued for at least six years.

It is also hard to believe that Lady Bird was not upset by Johnson's affairs, which, with the exception of the one with Alice Glass, were carried on with little concern for secrecy, but however troubled she may have been, she never showed it.

Even when she was asked about evidence that made Johnson's misbehavior undeniable, she reacted by saying, "Lyndon loved people. It would be unnatural for him to withhold love from half the people." On another occasion, she remarked, "I guess I'm used to it, 'cause I like for women to like him, and I like him to like them." Johnson's longtime aide Horace Busby explained, "The key to understanding Lady Bird is to understand that in her mind, her father was the role model for how all men are and should be. [That is] why she put up with LBJ's womanizing. . . . She grew up with her father and assumed all men had a wife but also had girlfriends."

The petite secretary later married a White House aide and remained a close family friend of the Johnsons. She speaks warmly of both Lady Bird and Lyndon to this day, and Lady Bird liked her enough to ask her to join Lady Bird's 1964 campaign rail trip through the South.

Still another factor in Lady Bird's tolerance of Johnson's misbehavior was that she enjoyed the excitement her husband brought to their lives. For many Washington wives of the era, being at the center of the action made it worth indulging considerable misbehavior by the husbands. And, for at least the last twenty years of their marriage, Johnson knew that he needed his wife's care and counsel, and she knew that he needed both.

In 1955, her care played a major role in Johnson's recovery.

But there's also no question that the new affair helped bring new zest to his life.

Another factor in his recovery, a rebirth of his dream of the White House, was inspired by the columnist Holmes Alexander, who proclaimed Johnson still to be a leading presidential candidate. Johnson's dream gained further encouragement when Dwight Eisenhower suffered a heart attack even more serious than his. Johnson then threw himself into a frenzy of political activity.

Adlai Stevenson and Sam Rayburn were invited to Johnson's ranch, ostensibly so the three men could assure the nation that the Democrats would not seek political advantage from the president's illness. In reality, Johnson let Rayburn know that he wanted to seek the presidency, and he gave Stevenson political advice designed to ease Johnson's path.

He urged Stevenson to run against Estes Kefauver in the 1956 Democratic primaries, secretly hoping that the two would force a deadlock so that the Democratic convention would then turn to Johnson. This advice could be taken to confirm that Johnson had read Machiavelli's *The Prince*, a copy of which the columnist Mary McGrory had spotted on his hospital bed—though it could be argued that Johnson's career had already demonstrated that he might be able to teach Machiavelli a few tricks rather than the other way around.

After Johnson's return to Washington in November 1955, the financier and former ambassador Joseph P. Kennedy sent word to him through Tommy Corcoran that he would finance Johnson's presidential campaign if Johnson would take Kennedy's son Senator John F. Kennedy as his running mate. Johnson rejected the offer, because he thought Joe's true goal was for Johnson to lose, clearing the way for Jack Kennedy to emerge as the logical Democratic nominee in 1960.

In the event, Johnson's presidential machinations proved

fruitless. Stevenson won the nomination, and at the convention he left the choice of vice president to the delegates. Estes Kefauver, who had impressed the nation with his Senate hearings that had revealed the power of the mafia, and John Kennedy, who had impressed the delegates with his nominating speech for Stevenson, became the main contenders. In what would prove to be the last exciting ballot at a Democratic National Convention, the vote seesawed back and forth between the two before Kefauver finally emerged the victor. In the fall, Eisenhower, who had recovered from his heart attack, swamped the Stevenson-Kefauver ticket.

The good news for Johnson was that he was now free to concentrate on his duties as majority leader, the Democrats having retained control of the Senate despite the Eisenhower landslide.

What followed in 1957 was what many believe to be his most impressive legislative accomplishment, the first civil rights bill to pass the Congress since the days of Reconstruction. For eight decades, the majority of Americans had accepted racial segregation in the South. Indeed, movies, from their beginning through the early 1940s, had portrayed blacks as happily working as servants and, in one major movie, even joyously singing the Confederate anthem "Dixie." The Supreme Court, since *Plessy v. Ferguson*, decided in 1896, had blessed separate schools and other facilities as long as they were equal, but it had devoted precious little effort to enforcing "equal."

During World War II, however, President Roosevelt's Fair Employment Practices Commission had greatly expanded job opportunities for blacks, often placing them in jobs in which they worked alongside whites. Although a conservative Congress killed the FEPC after the war, the cause of equality had been advanced—as it was again when Harry Truman desegregated the armed forces in 1948. In the late 1940s, Hollywood was making movies such as *Pinky* that attacked racial bigotry.

The black writer James Baldwin published his first novel, and other books and magazine and newspaper articles expressing concern about racial injustice appeared.

But far and away the most important development came in 1954 when in *Brown v. Board of Education* the Supreme Court outlawed racial segregation in the public schools. The decision took years to carry out, and its implementation was, to put it gently, imperfect. Nevertheless, it represented a landmark declaration by the nation's highest court that racial segregation was wrong.

In December 1955, on a bus in Montgomery, Alabama, a black woman named Rosa Parks refused to surrender her seat to a white person. After she was arrested and jailed, she and her cause were embraced by a young black preacher who had assumed the pulpit of the Dexter Avenue Baptist Church just the year before. His name was Martin Luther King Jr. "There comes a time," he declared, "when people get tired of being trampled over by the iron feet of oppression."

King became the leader of a movement to desegregate the Montgomery buses. The movement chose the nonviolent tactic of boycott as King shamed white Christians with his example of applied Christianity. When King's house was bombed, and non-violence was met with the violence of the white supremacists, blacks were joined by white liberals and moderates in their outrage, outrage that had begun to stir in the summer of 1955, when a fourteen-year-old black boy from Chicago named Emmett Till was murdered because he had whistled at a white woman.

King was hailed as a national leader of the civil rights movement, invited to speak at a San Francisco convention of the NAACP (National Association for the Advancement of Colored People) and in 1956 to the platform committee of the Democratic National Convention in Chicago. Men and women, black and white, all over the country, found themselves inspired by him.

By 1957 it was clear to Johnson that not only had the time for congressional action on civil rights arrived, but if he was to have any hope of becoming president the time had also arrived for him to separate himself from his segregationist southern colleagues in the Senate.

If a civil rights bill was to pass, it needed Democratic votes. The Republicans remained enough of the party of Lincoln, out of either conviction or a desire to embarrass the Democrats and win black votes, for a majority of Republican senators to support the bill. But that majority was still a minority in the Senate.

Within his own party, Johnson faced the obstacle not only of southern solidarity but of western senators who needed southern votes for their major legislative goal that year, a bill authorizing the Hells Canyon Dam on the Snake River.

One part of the civil rights bill, called Title III, would have desegregated all public facilities, including hotels and restaurants. Since this would end the separation of the races that had become the essence of southern culture, it was the element of the bill that was hardest for the South to swallow.

Another part of the bill, however, was more difficult for conservatives to oppose, since to do so they would have to justify denying the vote to citizens. Nevertheless, they feared the political power that the vote would give their black constituents.

How could the southerners avoid seeming to deny African Americans a basic right and yet maintain their power? The answer was an amendment requiring all cases of criminal contempt—cases that would, for example, be brought against officials who refused to register blacks—to be tried by a jury. Southern jurors, the conservative senators realized, could be counted on to protect the existing order.

Johnson wanted a bill that could pass. So he abandoned Title III and its desegregation of public facilities. He also wanted to accept the jury amendment to neutralize southern opposition. But here he ran into opposition from liberal northern Democrats who were convinced that the jury amendment would render the bill toothless.

Johnson could not win without at least some northern liberal votes. Senator Frank Church of Idaho came to his rescue with a proposal to amend the amendment by requiring that the juries be desegregated instead of being all white, as had been the custom in the South.

Johnson immediately saw the beauty of Church's idea and proceeded to stage a debate on the Senate floor designed to win over enough liberals to pass the bill.

It began with a speech by Senator Joseph O'Mahoney of Wyoming advocating the jury trial amendment: "Denial of the right of trial by jury will only make matters worse than they are, for the trial by jury for criminal offenses is a right guaranteed to every citizen."

Senator Church asked, "Will the Senator yield?" O'Mahoney had known and approved of Church's idea before taking the floor, but his colleagues were unaware of that fact. He feigned surprise at Church's interruption, and with seeming reluctance agreed to yield the floor for two minutes. Church introduced his "desegregate the jury" amendment to the jury amendment, explaining that it was "designed to eliminate whatever basis there may be for the charge that the efficacy of the trial by jury is weakened by the fact that in some areas, colored citizens are prevented from serving as jurors."

O'Mahoney played the part of the open-minded legislator who immediately saw the obvious merit of a colleague's suggestion, and he declared himself "happy to accept" it.

Then another of Johnson's role players, John Pastore of Rhode Island, rose to perform the role of "the doubter," expressing to O'Mahoney every reservation that liberals had to the jury amendment. Patiently, O'Mahoney dealt with each doubt, and Pastore faithfully portrayed a man not easily persuaded, once saying, "I think the Senator from Wyoming is moving a little too quickly." But gradually, very gradually, Pastore yielded to the force of O'Mahoney's logic and finally pronounced himself thoroughly convinced, with the Church amendment acting as the clincher.

Observers credited this colloquy with persuading enough senators to support the amendment as amended. But to make doubly sure, Johnson arranged for senators to receive telegrams from the presidents of twelve railroad brotherhoods endorsing it. The brotherhoods were especially powerful in the western states whose senators Johnson needed.

On August 2, the Senate voted. When Vice President Nixon announced the tally, it was 51 in favor of the amendment, 42 against. The Church amendment had done its job, winning over six liberals, including John F. Kennedy of Massachusetts.

But outside the Senate, many liberal and black leaders were angry. Even with the Church amendment, they realized that there would still be enough whites on each jury to keep it from convicting a white official. The black baseball star Jackie Robinson sent Eisenhower a telegram urging him not to approve the bill. A. Philip Randolph, the head of the Brotherhood of Sleeping Car Porters, said, "It is worse than no bill at all." The civil rights attorney Joseph Rauh said, "I was so mad at Johnson I was speechless."

But Johnson knew what buttons to push with Rauh. He called a mutual friend, Phil Graham, the publisher of the *Washington Post*, and asked him to help turn Rauh around. Graham had a persuasive argument to convince Rauh. Getting Congress on record that African Americans should have the right to vote, he said, was more important than the bill's imperfections.

As Senator Kennedy put it, the bill "represents an almost

universal acknowledgment that we cannot continue to command the respect of people everywhere, not to mention our own self respect, while we ignore the fact that many of our citizens do not possess basic constitutional rights."

Rauh was persuaded. He in turn persuaded Roy Wilkins of the NAACP with the argument that "once Congress had lost its virginity on civil rights, it would go on to make up what had been lost."

Wilkins then persuaded other civil rights organizations to join in a statement declaring, "Disappointing as the Senate's version is, it does contain some potential good" and should be enacted.

Johnson was overjoyed. The final bill passed 72–18. Only one liberal Democrat opposed it, and, more significantly, five southern senators supported it—Ralph Yarborough of Texas, George Smathers of Florida, Albert Gore Sr. and Estes Kefauver of Tennessee, and, of course, Johnson himself.

A key element in the bill's passage was Richard Russell's refusal to lead a filibuster against it. He persuaded all of his southern colleagues, except Strom Thurmond, that if the South tried to filibuster, it would lose a cloture vote to cut off debate. Thurmond's biographer Nadine Cohodas writes that he "remained convinced that Russell was motivated more by a desire to help Lyndon Johnson pass a civil rights bill—and thereby boost the Texan's presidential hopes—than a wish to protect the South." Since, on the key vote that ensured passage of the bill, on the O'Mahoney amendment as amended by Church, Johnson was able to muster only 51 votes, it's hard to see where he would have gotten the two-thirds necessary to halt debate in 1957. In other words, Thurmond was probably right about Russell's motivation.

The bill's passage was hailed by the nation's media, and Lyndon Johnson got the credit. A headline in the *Washington*

Post proclaimed it "Johnson's Masterpiece." And in *The Reporter*, a moderately liberal magazine that was quite influential in the 1950s, Douglass Cater called it "the most remarkable feat of political generalship in years" and concluded, "Johnson is a spectacular operator."

It is hard to overstate the regard with which technical skill was valued in the 1950s. Society didn't hesitate to forgive the prominent New Deal lawyers Tommy Corcoran, Thurman Arnold, and Paul Porter for leaving public service to sell their skills to the highest bidder in private practice. The skills were admired even more than the cause they served. In fact, high skill, whatever cause it served, was admired. At no time in modern history have the geniuses of the advertising world been more esteemed. Even exposés of their misdeeds, like the 1947 film *The Hucksters*, romanticized them with the hero Clark Gable "forced" to choose between Ava Gardner and Deborah Kerr. As for politicians, Johnson's friend the *New York Times* and *Harper's* writer William White wrote a book called *The Professional*, which extolled the legislative skill of Lyndon Johnson.

Although it is fair to point out that Johnson shared a number of characteristics with the manipulators of Madison Avenue, it should be added in his defense that he wasn't using his legislative wizardry to sell cigarettes. Most of the bills he guided through the Senate had at least some merit.

The Civil Rights Act of 1957 largely failed to achieve its main objective, which was to give the vote to black Americans. Wily southern judges and registrars found ways to avoid and evade the new law. And Eisenhower's Department of Justice proved to be an unenthusiastic enforcer. Still, to anyone who lived through the 1950s aware of the decade's profound resistance to liberal ideas and social change, the bill was a stunning achievement for Johnson. He got Congress on record in favor of giving the vote to blacks.

During the final years of the 1950s, Johnson devoted most of his efforts to exploring why America had fallen behind in the space race. The Soviet Union launched its Sputniks, first circling the globe with a satellite, then with a dog, and finally with the first man in space. Too often, American attempts to reach outer space seemed to end with the missiles exploding on the launchpad.

Johnson held hearings that spotlighted the Eisenhower administration's failures, hearings that led to the enactment of legislation authorizing the National Aeronautics and Space Administration, or NASA. In doing so, he not only gave his party an issue that could be used against the Republicans in the 1960 election, he positioned the country to become the world's leader in space.

5

Running Second

One day toward the end of April 1960, a local lawyer who had joined the presidential campaign of Senator John F. Kennedy happened to have business to transact at the assessor's office in Kanawha County, West Virginia. One of the women who worked there whispered in his ear, "A Washington lawyer named James Rowe just gave Sam [the assessor] $10,000 to use for Humphrey." Rowe was not for Humphrey but for his old friend Lyndon Johnson. He was helping Humphrey in the hope that the Protestant Humphrey would defeat the Catholic Kennedy in West Virginia, a state whose population was 95 percent Protestant, and thereby open Johnson's path to the presidency.

This illustrated a major problem with Lyndon Johnson's campaign strategy in pursuing the 1960 Democratic presidential nomination. The money was too little and too late. The Kennedys had already locked up the county's dominant faction. And Johnson, instead of openly campaigning for himself, was relying on surrogates such as Hubert Humphrey and Adlai Stevenson to deadlock the Democratic Convention, which he hoped would then turn to him because of his impressive record as Senate majority leader and his friendship with powerful Democratic senators who would use their influence with delegates from their states to win the nomination.

In West Virginia, for example, Senator Robert Byrd was known to be for Johnson. But what Johnson failed to understand was that Byrd needed local leaders like Judge Sidney Christie of McDowell County more than they needed him. If Judge Christie wanted to support Kennedy, Byrd could not order him to switch to Humphrey—or later to Johnson—and risk offending Christie and losing his help when Byrd next ran for reelection. After all, Judge Christie's endorsement usually meant his candidate would win the county by at least 10,000 votes.

The other problem with Johnson's strategy was that with Humphrey knocked out of serious contention by his landslide loss to Kennedy in West Virginia on May 9 and with Adlai Stevenson refusing to commit himself to running despite Johnson's importuning, the prospect for a deadlocked convention seemed dim indeed. By most counts, Kennedy was only a handful of votes shy of a majority and appeared on the verge of clinching the nomination as the convention delegates gathered in Los Angeles in mid-July.

Still Johnson clung to the hope, even though he realized it was slim, that he might somehow emerge as the nominee. On Monday and Tuesday as the convention was getting under way, he visited one state delegation after another, pressing the flesh and making speeches. But too many delegates were already committed to Kennedy. Johnson realized he had to gamble on a long shot.

He challenged Kennedy to debate before the combined Texas and Massachusetts delegations, confident that he could outargue his young opponent and hoping that his victory might be sufficiently overwhelming to sweep him to the nomination.

The Kennedy camp was reluctant to afford Johnson this last chance but realized that Jack might appear cowardly if he ducked the challenge.

Besides, in West Virginia, Kennedy had surprised his supporters, and one suspects even himself, by winning a debate against the Democrats' best debater, Hubert Humphrey. So Kennedy had reason to believe that he could at least hold his own. During the debate, Johnson attacked Kennedy for his absenteeism from the Senate, noting that, while he himself had attended all quorum calls in one ten-day period, "some" senators had attended none.

Kennedy replied that he assumed Johnson was talking about some other senators and proceeded to praise Johnson's record of "answering those quorum calls." According to the *New York Herald Tribune*, Kennedy "lauded Senator Johnson's skill in the Senate, and his record in passing bills, concluding that he firmly supported Lyndon Johnson—as majority leader." The *Trib*'s report, written by Rowland Evans Jr., concluded, "After Sen. Kennedy's brief effective reply, no one here tonight was counting on a sudden surge of new votes for the Texan."

Kennedy had outclassed Johnson. It was the kind of experience that would create a lasting mixture of resentment, admiration, and insecurity in Johnson's relationship with Kennedy—and the fact that it happened in front of his home folks from Texas made it especially galling.

Johnson had two arguments against Kennedy that he did not use in the debate. One actually was against the Massachusetts senator's father. During a speech to the Washington state delegation, for example, Johnson declared, "I wasn't any Chamberlain-umbrella policy man," referring to Joe Kennedy's advocacy of appeasing Hitler when the senior Kennedy was U.S. ambassador to Great Britain in the late 1930s. And Johnson's allies, including John Connally and India Edwards, leaked word to reporters that Jack Kennedy suffered from Addison's disease, a debilitating autoimmune disorder of the adrenal glands. This enraged Kennedy's brother and campaign manager Robert, who reportedly told Bobby Baker, "You Johnson people are running a stinking damned campaign and you're gonna get yours when the time comes."

Robert Kennedy was already far from being a fan of Johnson's. And if admiration was among a complex of feelings Johnson had for Jack Kennedy, it was no part of his response to Bobby, who often seemed abrasive, a characteristic not likely to beguile anyone steeped in the traditions of southern and senatorial courtesy. Indeed, Martin F. Nolan, the veteran Washington correspondent of the *Boston Globe*, says "abrasive is an understatement." He cites an incident from a few years later, when Bobby sought the support of the Senate minority leader, Everett Dirksen, for a measure he favored. According to Nolan, when Dirksen hesitated, Bobby immediately attacked, saying, "You've always hated the Kennedys, haven't you?" This left the courtly senator, who was genuinely fond of both Jack and Teddy, more than a little taken aback.

That spring, Jack Kennedy had sent Bobby to Texas to find out whether Johnson was running for president. Johnson lied, saying he wasn't. He then dragooned Bobby into a deer hunt, equipping him with a high-powered shotgun. Its recoil knocked Bobby down and cut his eye.

"Son, you've got to learn to handle a gun like a man," Johnson commented.

On Wednesday of the convention week in Los Angeles, Bobby got his revenge, as his brother walloped Johnson, winning the nomination, 806 votes to 409.

Bobby did not have long to gloat, however. The next morning John Kennedy decided to offer Johnson the vice presidential nomination. He had been leaning toward Johnson, although many of his more liberal supporters favored Senator Stuart Symington of Missouri. And Jack knew that Bobby had promised such liberals as the labor leader Walter Reuther and the NAACP's Roy Wilkins that Johnson would not be the vice president.

Still, as early as Monday, when the *Washington Post* publisher Phil Graham and columnist Joe Alsop told him that Johnson would be the best choice for vice president, Jack told them that he agreed. On Tuesday, the *Post* reported that Johnson would be Kennedy's choice.

Kennedy, however, did not want to make an offer that Johnson might refuse. He decided to use a back channel to gauge Johnson's interest. He asked Thomas P. "Tip" O'Neill, a Massachusetts congressman and Kennedy loyalist who was also close to Sam Rayburn, to talk to the Speaker. Rayburn sent back word that Johnson would accept the nomination if it was offered.

On the morning after the presidential balloting, Lady Bird answered the phone in Johnson's suite at the Biltmore Hotel. She said, "Lyndon, it's Senator Kennedy. He wants to talk to you."

Kennedy, who had rooms on an upper floor at the same hotel, said he was sending Bobby down to Johnson's suite. Bobby, temporarily stifling his own reservations, told Johnson that his brother wanted him to be his running mate. Johnson said he needed time to consider the offer but indicated he was favorably disposed.

Why would Johnson give up his seemingly immense power as majority leader to accept the historical impotence of the vice presidency? The most likely explanation is that he saw it as the only way a southerner could get to the White House. This was the point that George Reedy had made in a preconvention memo to Johnson and that Johnson himself made to Clare Boothe Luce, the influential writer and wife of the publisher of

Time and *Life*, when she asked him why he would even consider giving up being majority leader.

At 10 a.m. Jack Kennedy called and read Johnson the press release that he and his advisers had drafted, announcing Johnson as his choice.

"Do you really want me?" Johnson asked.

Kennedy said yes, and Johnson accepted.

As word leaked out that Kennedy was choosing Johnson, party liberals rebelled, protesting vehemently to both Jack and Bobby. At 1:30 p.m. Bobby went to Johnson's suite and asked Johnson if he would accept the chairmanship of the Democratic National Committee instead of the vice presidency. Sam Rayburn said, "Aw, shit!" Phil Graham called Jack, who told him, "Bobby's been out of touch and doesn't know what's happening." Kennedy then talked to Johnson, reiterating his desire to have him on the ticket. Ruffled feathers were smoothed and the press release was finally issued.

It is difficult, if not impossible, for anyone who knew the Kennedys to believe that Bobby's offer of the party chairmanship had been made without Jack's approval. What seems likely is that Jack did okay the attempt, but when Phil Graham made it clear that the ploy had failed, Kennedy realized he could not risk alienating the South by jettisoning Johnson and decided he had to stand by his original offer.

Some of the liberals went along. But others, most notably Joe Rauh, continued to resist Johnson. That night, Rauh could be seen striding around the convention hall, stirring up opposition. He was having enough success that the Kennedy forces decided that having a ballot might be embarrassing. So they had John McCormack, the House majority leader, and another Massachusetts politician, move for a voice vote. When the convention chairman called for the voice vote, it was hard for most observers to tell whether the yeas or nays prevailed. But the chairman declared Johnson the winner.

Johnson was the vice presidential nominee. Now he had to deliver on his supporters' promise that he would carry the South for Kennedy in his race against Vice President Richard Nixon.

Kennedy had two problems in the South: race and religion. The convention had adopted the most liberal civil rights plank in the party's history. Johnson's role was to signal to his fellow southerners that Kennedy would be reasonable in carrying out the policy advocated by the platform. As for religion, Johnson took the issue on directly.

Speaking at the Alamo in San Antonio on September 12, he asked how anyone could question the patriotism of Catholics, pointing out that at the Alamo, "side by side with Bowie and Crockett, died McCafferty, Bailey, and Carey, but no one knows whether they were Catholics or not. For there was no religious test at the Alamo."

From the platform of his campaign train, Johnson told the story of how Kennedy's older brother, Joe Jr., had a copilot from New Braunfels, Texas, when their plane went down in the English Channel: "I'm sure that they didn't ask each other what church they went to. They both died for their country." The five-day train tour through the South was mostly a success for Johnson. Advanced by a team of five women—"What Southern gentleman is not going to receive Southern ladies when they are coming to his city?" remarked Lindy Boggs, the wife of Representative Hale Boggs of Louisiana—the train arrived and departed from each town with its loudspeakers blaring "The Yellow Rose of Texas." Lady Bird, Luci, and Lynda joined Johnson on the platform and posed for pictures with local politicians. Johnson tailored his remarks to fit each locality. "What has Nixon ever done for Culpeper, Virginia?" he asked the citizens of that small town.

But the greatest triumph of Johnson's campaign came amid a scene rich with the promise of political disaster. On the afternoon that he and Lady Bird reached the Baker Hotel in Dallas, they had to shoulder their way through a booing and hissing right-wing mob, carrying signs with messages reading "LBJ Sold Out to Yankee Socialists."

That night the Johnsons had to cross the street to the Adolphus Hotel, where he was scheduled to speak. Again, they had to make their way through a hostile mob. One woman grabbed Lady Bird's gloves and threw them into the gutter. The crowd chanted "Judas" and "traitor."

Johnson refused a police escort, saying, "If the time has come when I can't walk through the lobby of a hotel in Dallas with my lady without a police escort, I want to know it."

Many southerners who took pride in their good manners were repelled by the mob scenes, and the dignity with which the Johnsons bore the ordeal won them enormous sympathy.

Even though Johnson's campaigning was mostly effective, he worried himself sick about the possibility of failing in his mission to carry the South for the Kennedy-Johnson ticket. Johnson had always been a demanding boss. But now he berated his staff for the most minor mishaps, causing even the loyal Jim Rowe to quit the campaign. He wrote Johnson: "I have not seen you pay one compliment, thank one person, be the sweet and kind and attractive Lyndon I used to know in all the time I have traveled with you. I have seen you do nothing but yell at them, every single one of them. . . . The morale of your staff is awful."

For Johnson's staff, this was a foretaste of things to come as his anxieties about Vietnam would produce long stretches of similar meanness. But this time his worries were groundless. He did not fail.

On November 8, the Kennedy-Johnson ticket carried not only Texas but Georgia, North Carolina, South Carolina, Alabama,

Louisiana, and Arkansas as well. Johnson had done his job, making a major contribution to John Kennedy's comfortable majority in the electoral college when Kennedy's popular margin was fewer than 130,000 votes. And now Johnson was vice president of the United States.

As he assumed the vice presidency, Lyndon Johnson made two attempts to ensure that he would be a powerful player instead of fading into the obscurity that had been the fate of most vice presidents.

First, he tried to get Democratic senators to let him preside over their caucus. But enough of his former colleagues, led by Senator Albert Gore Sr., voted against the proposal that it was clear to Johnson he was not wanted. His response to the rebuff: "Now I know the difference between a caucus and a cactus. In a cactus all the pricks are on the outside."

He was equally unsuccessful in securing John Kennedy's approval for a memo asking for an executive order giving Johnson "general supervision" over several government agencies and ordering department heads to provide him with copies of all documents sent to Kennedy. The White House staff leaked the memo to the press, which embarrassed Johnson almost as much as Kennedy's failure to reply to it.

Still, Kennedy wanted to keep Johnson inside the tent. "I can't afford to have my vice president, who knows every reporter in Washington, going around saying we're all screwed up," he told his trusted political aide Ken O'Donnell.

To make Johnson feel good, Kennedy gave him a six-room suite in the Old Executive Office Building next to the White House. Johnson's Senate colleagues also sought to soothe his ego by letting him keep his majority leader's quarters, Capitol Hill's grandest offices, often referred to as the "Taj Mahal." In addition, Kennedy invited Johnson to attend cabinet meetings and presidential get-togethers with Senate and House leaders.

Kennedy also asked Johnson to chair the National Aeronautics and Space Council and to head the Committee on Equal Employment Opportunity. Johnson had, of course, been an original sponsor of the legislation creating NASA, and Kennedy viewed him as a southern moderate who would be valuable in advancing the cause of equal job opportunities for blacks.

Kennedy also tried to protect Johnson's dignity. He instructed his chief of protocol, Angier Biddle Duke, to make sure that the Johnsons always received special treatment at ceremonial occasions, and he told O'Donnell, who in addition to being a political adviser often served as unofficial chief of the White House staff: "You're dealing with a very insecure, sensitive man with a huge ego. I want you literally to kiss his ass from one end of Washington to the other." Despite this injunction, however, it was well known in Washington that there were those in the White House who were not reluctant to ridicule the vice president in private.

Kennedy's main method of dealing with Johnson was to keep him busy sending him on missions abroad. Most of the trips were ceremonial, but two turned out to be important.

Johnson went to Germany at a crucial moment in its history—just after the Communists had erected the Berlin Wall and Germans were afraid they might be deserted by the United States. Johnson told a crowd of three hundred thousand Berliners that we would stand by them with the same commitment "our ancestors pledged in forming the United States: 'our lives, our fortunes, and our sacred honor.'" This was an early expression of post-Korea U.S. policy. America was going to respond to Communist provocation not by attacking East Berlin but by making clear that we would defend non-Communist West Berlin.

The other significant Johnson trip—to South Vietnam—was important for another reason. It was where he first formed the conviction that would later lead to tragedy. On his return, he told Kennedy, "I cannot stress too strongly the extreme importance of following up this mission with other measures, other actions, and other efforts. . . . we must decide whether to help these countries [Vietnam and its neighbors in Southeast Asia] to the best of our ability or throw in the towel in the area and pull back our defenses to San Francisco and a 'Fortress America' concept."

In April 1961, John Kennedy did not involve Johnson in the White House decision on the Bay of Pigs, the CIA-sponsored invasion of Cuba by Cuban exiles that proved to be a disastrous failure. Instead, he kept Johnson busy entertaining West German chancellor Konrad Adenauer at the LBJ ranch.

Eighteen months later, during the Cuban Missile Crisis, in which the United States faced the threat of nuclear-armed missiles being stationed in Cuba by the Russians, Kennedy did invite Johnson to take part in the Executive Committee of the National Security Council (EXCOMM), the top-secret meetings that Kennedy held with his senior advisers. Johnson's participation, however, proved modest. In fact, John and Robert Kennedy (who was now the attorney general) were heard to complain about Johnson's failure to speak up more often or to take a firm stand. Johnson said little, but what he did contribute displayed the same kind of wavering between hawk and dove that the president himself experienced, only Johnson ended up firmly on the hawk side while Kennedy tended more toward looking tough but being dovish. Johnson's last words as he left the final meeting of EXCOMM were, "When I was a boy in Texas, and walking down the road when a rattlesnake reared up, the only thing you could do was take a stick and chop its head off." Instead, the Kennedys chose a nonviolent course that induced Soviet premier Nikita Khrushchev to withdraw the missiles voluntarily.

The early 1960s also saw the full flowering of one of the most remarkable movements in American history. Led by young African American students who sat at whites-only lunch counters and by the clergyman Martin Luther King Jr., whose following had grown dramatically since the Montgomery bus boycott in 1955, the movement had won increasing respect from white America because of its moral vision and nonviolent tactics. Pictures in newspapers and on television of blacks being beaten because they had attempted to ride on buses through the South and, most of all, of children being attacked by police dogs and fire hoses in Birmingham, Alabama, incensed the nation.

Kennedy's first response to the clamor against segregation was to create by executive order the Committee on Equal Employment Opportunity, to which he had named Johnson chairman. Now it was Johnson's job to carry out the CEEO's mission of eliminating racial discrimination in federal government employment and in hiring federal contractors. Although Johnson believed in this objective, the commission's method of achieving it was by seeking voluntary compliance, an approach that many black leaders believed was doomed. Chuck Stone, the editor of the *Washington Afro-American*, denounced the effort. Still, by the mid-1960s, the number of blacks in top federal jobs had increased by 35 percent, and in midlevel jobs by 22 percent.

With contractors, however, the record was not nearly so impressive. Only 40 percent of discrimination complaints against contractors were resolved in favor of the complainant, as compared to 76 percent in the case of the federal government.

Bobby Kennedy, a member of the commission, was critical of

Johnson. "The CEEO . . . could have been an effective organization," he declared, "if the vice president gave it some direction."
But Bobby's brother was not providing much direction himself.

John Kennedy worried about keeping his share of the southern vote in 1964 and was slow to react to the growing demand
for action from African Americans. But after Birmingham, in
June 1963 he proposed a new civil rights bill and made an
impassioned address to the nation. "We are confronted primarily with a moral issue," Kennedy said. "It is as old as the scrip-
tures and is as clear as the American Constitution. The heart of
the question is whether all Americans are to be afforded equal
rights and equal opportunities, whether we are going to treat
our fellow Americans as we want to be treated."

Still, neither the Kennedy brothers nor Lyndon Johnson
participated in King's March on Washington in August 1963,
where he delivered his inspiring "I have a dream" speech.
Indeed, they had advised against holding the event, a position
shared by most of white Washington, which embarrassed itself
by staying home that day. One of the few offices with all hands
on board was the Peace Corps headquarters. A few members of
the staff walked down through the Ellipse to Constitution Avenue, where suddenly appeared an immense crowd marching
peacefully along. The dust stirred up by their feet made a
golden mist under the trees, a halo for a great moment in American history. Back in the White House, Kennedy and Johnson
were impressed by the dignity of the occasion. "He's damn
good," the president told his aides.

Johnson's performance in his other main assignment as vice
president, as chairman of the space council, impressed most
observers. He was influential in the choice of James Webb, who
proved to be a highly effective administrator of NASA. And he
urged Kennedy to make "manned exploration of the moon" a
national goal.

This counsel was rendered in the spring of 1961, just as Kennedy needed an exciting project to divert his people's attention from the recent disastrous invasion of Cuba. The president saw the desirability of changing the subject from the Bay of Pigs to the Sea of Tranquility and proposed to Congress that we put a man on the moon before the end of the decade.

Johnson, always mindful of his political base, helped make sure that the manned spacecraft center was located in Houston. And he reaped the popular reward of his association with NASA when his approval soared as John Glenn circled the globe three times in his space capsule.

Still, rumors began to be heard around Washington that Johnson would be implicated in scandal and that Kennedy would replace him on the Democratic ticket in 1964. The evidence against Johnson was slim, but the involvement of his name with two individuals of questionable character created an embarrassing aroma.

One, a colorful Texas con man named Billy Sol Estes, was obviously guilty of several dubious deals, some of which involved bilking the federal government. The only convincing evidence against Johnson was that he had lobbied the Department of Agriculture on Estes's behalf. Estes, however, accused him of complicity in a murder plot, a charge of which Johnson was completely cleared but that was serious enough to have made the front pages in a way that did not add luster to the vice president's reputation.

In another scandal, the star was Bobby Baker, the longtime Senate aide who had become secretary of the Senate and had attained enough power through wheeling and dealing to be called "the 101st senator." Baker's skill had made him invaluable to Johnson during his years as Senate majority leader, and the two men were known to be very close. Baker's children, in fact, were named Lynda and Lyndon Baines.

Johnson's friend Les Carpenter once said of Baker: "There are some people who like to look crooked even when they aren't. And Bobby was one of those characters. He would always do the simplest thing in such a way to make it look like a deep, dark plot that had been hatched in a back room with thousands of dollars laid on the table."

Finally, however, appearance came close to reality when a vending machine company accused Baker of having deprived it of a government contract when it wouldn't provide an adequate kickback. Baker was forced to resign from his Senate job.

Johnson's name came up when it was revealed that Baker had given the vice president an expensive stereo. Johnson acknowledged the gift but said that he "hardly knew Bobby Baker," a remark that did not improve Johnson's credibility.

Johnson worried enough about the danger to his name that he arranged for his friend Abe Fortas, the brilliant Washington lawyer who had won the legal victory that made Johnson a senator, to represent Baker. One aspect of Baker's life was doubtless of special concern to Johnson: Baker was known to be an authority on the subject of senators and their mistresses.

It is hard to believe that further inquiry by the press into this area of Baker's expertise was not a concern to John Kennedy as well as to Johnson. Both men had a well-known weakness for the opposite sex. And Kennedy had closely followed the Profumo scandal, in which the British minister of defense had been forced to resign because of his illicit affair with a call girl named Christine Keeler, whose other lovers included a Soviet military aide. Kennedy knew that J. Edgar Hoover had found out about his own affair with Ellen Rometsch, an attractive East German refugee who had been one of the many women associated with Bobby Baker. A recent story in the *New York Times* about how a New Orleans businessman had "partied" with Baker and Rometsch seems likely to have heightened Kennedy's anxiety. The degree of John Kennedy's concern is suggested by an unusually solicitous call that Robert Kennedy made to Baker as the scandal peaked. "My brother and I extend our sympathies to you," the attorney general said. "I know you'll come through this." In the event, however, no stories appeared linking Johnson or Kennedy to other girls.

Their shared concern in this matter may have created a bond between the two men that, along with Kennedy's desire to win the South, helped inspire the president not to dump Johnson from the ticket. Instead, in the fall of 1963, Kennedy turned to Johnson for help in healing a fight between Senator Ralph Yarborough and Governor John Connally for control of the Democratic Party in Texas. Kennedy believed that repairing the breach between the two men was essential to the party winning Texas in the 1964 election. So a trip to Texas was planned, and Kennedy asked Johnson to go with him.

On November 21, John and Jacqueline Kennedy, accompanied by Lyndon and Lady Bird, arrived in Texas. The next morning, after the president spoke at a breakfast in Fort Worth, the two couples flew on Air Force One to Dallas, where they proceeded in a motorcade through the downtown business district.

Lyndon and Lady Bird occupied one car with Senator Yarborough beside them. Ahead, another car carried the president and first lady in the back seat with Governor Connally and his wife, Nellie, in the jump seats. The car's top had been removed at Kennedy's instruction so that it would be easier for people to see him.

Fears that conservative Texans would display hostility to Kennedy quickly dissipated as the crowd along the way greeted the president and his wife with cheers. Nellie Connally turned to Kennedy and said, "You can't say that Dallas doesn't love you."

As the motorcade left downtown, it passed the building housing the Texas School Book Depository. One of its employees, Lee Harvey Oswald, sat by a sixth-floor window holding a rifle with a telescopic site. He fired three shots. One shattered Kennedy's skull, making Lyndon Johnson the thirty-sixth president of the United States.

The mournful flight back to Washington aboard Air Force One exacerbated the tension between the Johnson and Kennedy camps. Trouble began even before takeoff. Kennedy's aides wanted to leave Dallas as soon as the dead president's casket had been loaded aboard. Johnson countermanded their instructions to the pilot. He felt he had to remain on the ground until a federal judge could be found and brought aboard to administer the oath of office.

For Johnson, taking the oath would remove any doubt about the legality of his ascension to the presidency. He was convinced that Robert Kennedy, who, after all, was the attorney general, had told him as much in a phone conversation soon after the assassination. Kennedy remembered otherwise and was outraged that his grieving sister-in-law had been made to wait for more than an hour before she could bring her husband home.

Finally, Judge Sarah Hughes of the federal district court arrived and administered the oath, which Johnson took with Jacqueline Kennedy at his side. Air Force One then took off. Lady Bird tried to comfort Jackie, but she proved inconsolable as she sat numbly still wearing the suit that had been soaked with her husband's blood.

The late president's aides sat by his casket as the plane made its way back to Washington. They drank heavily and were overheard lamenting their lost leader and contrasting his grace and wit with his successor's conspicuous lack thereof. And it is hard to believe that all the Johnson staffers on the plane could conceal their satisfaction at attaining the White House, where they would now hold sway over the Kennedy group that had been so condescending toward them.

When Air Force One arrived at Andrews Air Force Base, Bobby Kennedy rushed aboard. Anxious to get to Jacqueline as quickly as possible, he brushed past the new president as if he were part of the furniture. This definitely did not go unnoticed by Johnson's friends.

Stories of Bobby's apparent rudeness and of the remarks by his staff quickly spread through the Johnson camp. Simultaneously, Kennedy loyalists were told of ugly statements supposedly made by members of the Johnson team.

That evening, John Kennedy's aides gathered at the Bethesda Naval Hospital, where his body was autopsied and prepared for burial. Ken O'Donnell and John Kennedy's air force aide Godfrey McHugh gave Robert Kennedy inflammatory accounts of Johnson's behavior on the plane—McHugh called it "obscene"— even though a neutral observer aboard Air Force One, *Newsweek*'s Charles Roberts, found Johnson's behavior above reproach, as did another journalist, Charles Bartlett, the mutual friend who had brought John and Jacqueline Kennedy together.

The next morning, Bobby arrived at the Oval Office to find his brother's rocking chair upside down in the hallway and John Kennedy's secretary Evelyn Lincoln in tears because Johnson had given her only until noon to vacate her office. Episodes like these, told and retold, and often exaggerated, by both the Johnson and the Kennedy camps, continued to poison relationships between the two men and many, but not all, members of their staffs.

Meanwhile, the nation was engulfed in grief. In the minds

and hearts of his countrymen, John Kennedy's death had greatly enhanced his virtues while minimizing his faults. If an election had been held that weekend, he would have swept every state. People wept unashamedly as they watched the story of his life told and retold on television and witnessed the ceremonial events culminating in his funeral on November 25.

In public, both the Johnson and the Kennedy families rose above their problems with each other and behaved with great dignity throughout the weekend, helping the American people get through the days of mourning.

On the second day after John Kennedy's burial, Johnson went to Capitol Hill to deliver a speech that was both moving and reassuring. Harking back to Kennedy's inaugural address, which ended, "Let us begin," Johnson concluded, "Let us continue," pledging that he would carry on Kennedy's policy.

Robert Kennedy told a friend, "People don't realize how conservative Lyndon really is." Few remarks better illustrate how much the two men misunderstood each other, for Johnson now proceeded to get more liberal legislation passed by the Congress than any president in American history other than Franklin Roosevelt.

But before proceeding to his new New Deal, Johnson had to deal with the rumors about the assassination that now swept the country and threatened to sow seeds of distrust that could cripple his presidency. Conspiracy theories abounded, spurred on by the fact that the assassin, Lee Harvey Oswald, had been murdered in the basement garage of the Dallas police headquarters by a nightclub owner named Jack Ruby. Many of the rumors involved the mafia or Fidel Castro or Jimmy Hoffa, and some even held Lyndon Johnson complicit.

To dispel the rumors, Johnson asked Chief Justice Earl Warren to head a commission to investigate the facts and give a public report of its findings. The commission found that Lee Harvey Oswald, acting alone, had killed the president, and that Jack Ruby, also acting alone, had killed Oswald, and that neither of them was part of a conspiracy. Subsequent investigations of the two murders have cast doubt on the thoroughness of the commission's effort but not on the validity of its conclusion.

6

A Winning Year

In 1964, Johnson laid the foundations of what he would christen the Great Society in a speech at the University of Michigan in May. Its first two building blocks came in the form of bills he steered through Congress that year, the Economic Opportunity Act, which created the War on Poverty, and the Civil Rights Act of 1964.

The passage of these bills was motivated in part by the complex of feelings stirred by the Kennedy assassination. The mixture of guilt, love, and the desire to "do something" experienced by so many Americans found expression in personal action as well as in greater acceptance of the liberal beliefs thought to have been held by the late president. A record number of young Americans applied for service in the Peace Corps. Support for strengthening civil rights grew from 38 percent in 1963 to 57 percent in 1964. Johnson demonstrated his awareness of these feelings by continuing to emphasize his desire to carry on Kennedy's programs.

The War on Poverty, authorized by the Economic Opportunity Act of 1964, had its roots in pilot programs undertaken by the president's council on juvenile delinquency established under

Kennedy. The 1964 civil rights bill began as legislation sponsored by Kennedy in the summer of 1963 after he had been shocked by pictures of Bull Connor's police dogs attacking black children on the streets of Birmingham. Sympathy for blacks had grown among white Americans who shared Kennedy's shock at Connor's tactics, who were further impressed by the nonviolent March on Washington in August 1963, and who were repelled by the Birmingham church bombing by white supremacists that killed four little black girls in September.

The 1964 civil rights bill opened restaurants and hotels to blacks and gave the attorney general the right to enforce school desegregation. Johnson felt a personal commitment to it. "As an emotional issue," he said, he knew it contained the seeds of rebellion on Capitol Hill, "not just over civil rights but over my entire legislative program." As a moral issue, however, he felt it could not be avoided. Johnson recalled the advice of the former Speaker of the House and vice president (and fellow Texan) John Nance Garner, "a good poker player," who "once told me that there comes a time in every leader's career when he has to put in all his stack. I decided to shove in all my stack on this vital measure."

Johnson's sincere moral convictions about civil rights found reinforcement in a practical political fear that he later explained to his biographer Doris Kearns Goodwin. "I knew that if I didn't get out in front on this issue [the liberals] would get me," he said. "I had to produce a civil rights bill that was even stronger than the one they'd have gotten if Kennedy had lived."

To make sure he and the liberals were together, Johnson enlisted Capitol Hill's most prominent liberal, Senator Hubert Humphrey of Minnesota, to lead the fight for the bill in the Senate, telling Humphrey to "call me whenever there's trouble or anything you want me to do."

Hardly a week went by without a public statement by Johnson in support of the bill. He implored organized labor and

African American leaders to go all out in promoting it. When Roy Wilkins asked him how he could suddenly be so ardent— after all, as majority leader, Johnson had opposed the public accommodations section of the 1957 civil rights bill—the president explained: "You will recognize the words I'm about to repeat: Free at last. Free at last. Thank God almighty I'm free at last." Johnson was quoting Martin Luther King Jr. to explain that his rise to national leadership had freed him from the limitations political reality imposed on a legislator from a southern state—something his critics never seemed to understand.

Johnson foresaw that the South would be liberated by an end to segregation, which was stifling its economic growth. And history has proved him correct. He also foresaw that the end of segregation would lead to a Republican ascendancy in the South, telling Bill Moyers that the civil rights bill would deliver "the South to the Republican Party for a long time to come." Fortunately for Johnson, however, the political impact came after 1964, when it was still a net advantage for him to be perceived as loyally carrying out Kennedy's programs, and as a truly national leader, rather than just a regional one.

In June, another event occurred that heightened public awareness of the need for progress in race relations. Three young civil rights workers—two northern whites (Andrew Goodman and Michael Schwerner) and one southern black (James Chaney)—were murdered in Philadelphia, Mississippi, where they were attempting to register blacks to vote.

In the meantime, a crucial senator had been won over by Johnson and Humphrey. He was Everett Dirksen, the Republican minority leader, a man known for his flowery rhetoric, spoken with a deep and mellifluous voice, and, more relevant to the moment, a remarkably shrewd political tactician.

Johnson had assigned Humphrey to woo Dirksen. Humphrey threw himself into the task with characteristic enthusiasm. (He later confided, "I would have kissed [his] ass on the Capitol steps.") Humphrey's stroking played a significant role in Dirksen's conversion. Equally important, however, was Dirksen's own political intelligence. He saw the historical imperative, telling the Senate: "Stronger than all the armies is an idea whose time has come. The time has come for equality."

The showdown in the Senate came on a 71–29 vote invoking cloture to end a filibuster by southern senators who had managed to prolong the debate for seventy-five days. That vote took place on June 11. A week later the Civil Rights Act of 1964 passed the Senate 73–27, and on July 2 it passed the House by a margin of 289–126. That evening, Johnson signed the bill in the East Room of the White House.

Johnson loved to present signing pens to guests at such ceremonies. Among the recipients this time were Robert Kennedy, Martin Luther King Jr., Hubert Humphrey, and Everett Dirksen.

After civil rights, Johnson's legislative program for 1964 gave major emphasis to stimulating economic growth and opportunity. Growth he sought through enacting the tax cut that had been proposed by John Kennedy the previous year. Ironically, opposition to the cut came primarily from Republicans, who in subsequent decades—especially under the leadership of Ronald Reagan and George W. Bush—would argue that reducing taxes encouraged economic growth. In 1964, however, Republicans were firm believers in fiscal responsibility. But then as later, tax cuts proved politically hard to resist. By the end of February, the tax reduction bill became the first major congressional victory of the Johnson administration, passing both houses by wide margins.

Republicans would later cite the Kennedy cut—so it came to be described even though it was passed under Johnson—as a precedent for their own tax reductions, leaving aside the inconvenient truth that the 1964 cut only reduced the top marginal tax rate to 70 percent, roughly twice the top rate under George W. Bush.

Johnson's other economic effort, christened the War on Poverty, had roots that ranged from his youth in rural Texas to the impact on John Kennedy of his campaign in West Virginia in 1960 to a book that helped mobilize public support for a major program to help the poor. That book, *The Other America*, written by Michael Harrington and published in 1962, received a laudatory review in the *New Yorker* by the eminent critic Dwight Macdonald. More people may have been influenced by the review than by the book, which was not exactly a page-turner, but the result was that the nation's intellectual elite began to focus on poverty and what to do about it.

By 1964 the elites' concern had spread to the broader public, and a national consensus developed that something had to be done. Determining exactly what that would be proved a more difficult challenge. In the end, three main programs emerged.

Head Start provided preschool education for poor children. This was by far the most popular of the proposals because it was so obvious that many of these children arrived at primary school woefully behind their peers.

The Job Corps, modeled on Franklin Roosevelt's Civilian Conservation Corps, was also popular, at least in its early days, especially among those old enough—and there were still a good many of them—to remember the CCC as one of the most successful New Deal programs.

Unlike the CCC, which was largely composed of rural youth with most of its camps located in rural areas, the Job Corps drew a large number of its recruits from urban ghettos and set up many of its training centers in cities. The combination of unruly trainees and newspapers ready to report their misdeeds tended to dim the program's luster as time went on.

Community Action, aimed at organizing the poor to participate in creating and running their own programs and in seeking
help from existing government services, proved to be the hardest sell of the War on Poverty. From the beginning, many politicians speculated it might threaten their own power. Johnson
himself was wary.

Richard Boone, Community Action's leading guru, had
worked for the president's council on juvenile delinquency, run
out of Robert Kennedy's Department of Justice and the origin of
the pilot programs that were models for Community Action.
This aroused Johnson's suspicion that Community Action would
be a power base for people more loyal to Kennedy than to himself. And Johnson and the politicians weren't the only skeptics.
Some thoughtful observers, who appreciated the desirability of
participation by the poor, foresaw that actually organizing them
into programs that worked would prove exceedingly difficult.
Nonetheless, by August 1964, Community Action and the other
components of the War on Poverty had won congressional
approval in the form of a bill establishing the Office of Economic Opportunity (OEO).

Johnson chose Sargent Shriver to head the program. Shriver
had proved himself by making the Peace Corps into a success
story, even though many (including Dwight Eisenhower) had
dismissed it as another children's crusade, characterized by
amateurism and misguided idealism. John Kennedy credited
Shriver with having turned a lemon into lemonade.

Johnson also knew something that the general public did
not. Despite the fact that Shriver was married to Robert Kennedy's sister, there was no love lost between Shriver and the
attorney general. Johnson would enjoy public credit for appointing a member of the Kennedy family while comforting himself
with the knowledge that Shriver would not go out of his way to
advance the interest of his brother-in-law.

Another factor in Shriver's appointment was the influence of Bill Moyers, now one of Johnson's closest aides in the White House. Moyers had been Shriver's deputy in the Peace Corps and had come to feel genuine admiration and affection for his boss. So his recommendation of Shriver for the OEO job was rooted in real conviction. But Moyers had another motive. In 1964, his own ambition was to be head of the Peace Corps. By putting Shriver in another job, he would open the way for himself. Johnson thwarted this plan by leaving Shriver as director of the Peace Corps while also appointing him to the helm of the OEO. Moyers was too valuable at the White House for Johnson to let him move elsewhere.

Johnson's triumphs in domestic policy in 1964 were accompanied by his first misstep in foreign policy, taking him down a road that would ultimately lead to tragedy. The subject was Vietnam. In 1954, as insurgents forced the French to abandon their former colony called French Indochina, an international conference was held in Geneva that divided Indochina into three countries—Laos, Cambodia, and Vietnam. Vietnam in turn was divided into a Communist north and non-Communist south, pending an election that might or might not lead to unification. But an election was never held. The Communists, under their leader Ho Chi Minh, having played a major role in the insurgency that forced the French out, felt they were entitled to take over all of Vietnam and soon launched an insurgency in the South to advance their cause.

The United States, following its post–World War II policy of containing Communism—with the post-Korea corollary of avoiding aggression of our own—did not attempt to drive the Communists from the North but did help the government of the South resist insurgents called the Viet Cong, first with material aid and then with military "advisers." John Kennedy increased the number of advisers, and his administration became increasingly involved in trying to strengthen the South Vietnamese government, which was riddled with corruption and inefficiency. Ultimately, Kennedy supported a coup in 1963 that resulted in the assassination of the South Vietnamese leader Ngo Dinh Diem but did not have the desired effect of a significant improvement of the government. Indeed, in the first half of 1964, the situation in South Vietnam seemed to be deteriorating, and there was a real danger that the North and the Viet Cong would prevail.

In the first months of his presidency, Lyndon Johnson's Vietnam policy could be summarized by one word: undecided. As he explained to Senator William Fulbright on March 2, 1964, he was torn. On the one hand, if we withdraw, "Vietnam will collapse, and the ripple effect will be felt throughout Southeast Asia, endangering independent governments in Thailand, Malaysia, and extending as far as India and Indonesia and the Philippines." On the other hand, "We can send Marines, à la Goldwater . . . but our men may well be bogged down in a long war."

Not wanting to take either risk in an election year, as reflected by his reference to his likely Republican rival, Senator Barry Goldwater, Johnson told Fulbright that for the time being, we should stick to "providing training and logistical support." In late May, he told Adlai Stevenson, "I shudder at getting too deeply involved there."

It is possible that Johnson may have been tailoring his comments to fit what he regarded as the dovish inclinations and intellectual pretensions of Fulbright and Stevenson. His formal language, "I shudder at" and "the ripple effect will be felt throughout Southeast Asia," suggest that his remarks may have been scripted for effect. Still, similar uncertainty is evident in his discussions about Vietnam with his mentor and friend Senator Richard Russell, with whom he always conversed in his natural, earthy style.

"I'd like to hear you talk a little bit," Johnson asked in a telephone call on May 27, 1964.

"It's the damn worst mess I ever saw," Russell replied. "I knew that we were going to get into this sort of mess when we went in there. And I don't see how we're ever going to get out of it. . . . I just don't know what to do."

"That's the way that I've been feeling for six months," Johnson said.

On August 2, however, a report received by the White House situation room forced Johnson's hand. It said that North Vietnamese torpedo boats had attacked the U.S. destroyer *Maddox*, patrolling off the coast of North Vietnam in the Gulf of Tonkin.

At first, Johnson's instinct was to downplay the significance of the attack. He knew that a couple of days earlier, on July 30, South Vietnamese forces, encouraged by American advisers, had raided nearby North Vietnamese coastal installations. Perhaps the North Vietnamese had mistakenly concluded that the *Maddox* was involved in the raid.

On the morning after the *Maddox* incident, Johnson described it to Robert Anderson, a former secretary of the Treasury under Eisenhower and a pillar of the moderate Republican establishment. "There have been some covert operations we've been carrying on—blowing up some bridges and things of that kind, roads and so forth, so I imagine they [the North Vietnamese] wanted to put a stop to it," the president said.

But then Anderson warned, "You're going to be running against a man who's a wild man [Barry Goldwater] on this subject. Any lack of firmness, he'll make up. . . . Whatever you can do to say, 'when they shoot at us . . . we're going to protect ourselves, we'll protect our boys.'"

Johnson was impressed by Anderson's advice. Later that day, when Secretary of Defense Robert McNamara urged the president to let the public know about the South Vietnamese raids, Johnson told McNamara to inform a few leaders on the Hill about the provocation, but cautioned, "I'd tell them awfully quiet though so they won't . . . be making a bunch of speeches. . . . I want to leave an impression on background . . . that we're going to be firm as hell."

McNamara understood where Johnson's mind was heading. He then recommended that Johnson tell his press secretary, George Reedy, to issue a statement saying that the president "personally ordered the Navy . . . to destroy any force that attacks our forces in international waters."

Johnson had decided that the South Vietnamese provocation of July 30 should be kept quiet. And so on August 4, when he heard that Senator Humphrey had mentioned the provocation in a television interview, Johnson was upset. The president called his adviser James Rowe, who was also a friend of Humphrey's, to complain that Humphrey had disclosed that "we have been carrying on some operations in that area . . . that's exactly what we *have* been doing . . . that damn fool ought to keep his goddam big mouth shut on foreign affairs, at least until the election is over . . . that can ruin a man mighty quick."

Johnson was threatening Humphrey: shut up about the provocation, or you won't be vice president. Since everyone knew that Humphrey was panting for Johnson to choose him as the Democratic vice presidential nominee, this was very tough talk indeed.

Now, recall that just a day earlier, on the morning of August 3, Johnson had made the same disclosure privately to Robert Anderson that he now condemned Humphrey for making in public. Anderson's comments had clearly made an impact. He had said that Johnson couldn't appear to be soft because softness was just what Barry Goldwater was accusing him of. Goldwater had just won the Republican nomination for president at the party's convention in San Francisco. One of the main tenets of his campaign was that we had to be tough in defending South Vietnam—even using atomic weapons if necessary. And his message about toughness, if not about atomic weapons, clearly was impressing Americans. According to recent polls, 58 percent said they did not approve of the administration's handling of Vietnam. The pollster Lou Harris had concluded, "Vietnam was clearly an issue working for Goldwater."

Goldwater's nomination represented a victory for conservative Republicans over the moderates, who had dominated the party's conventions from Wendell Willkie's nomination in 1940 through Thomas E. Dewey in 1944 and 1948 and Dwight Eisenhower in 1952 and 1956. Richard Nixon's nomination in 1960 had been supported by both wings of the party, but now, in 1964, Goldwater had humiliated Governor Nelson Rockefeller of New York, the leader of the moderates, and he and his views were clearly in ascendance. And he was uncompromising in his view that the Communists in Vietnam must be defeated.

In addition to Johnson's concern about criticism from Goldwater, he worried about the possibility of criticism from someone in his own party, in fact in his own administration. That someone was the attorney general, Robert Kennedy.

Johnson knew that in the minds of a good many liberal Democrats, Bobby was his martyred brother's legitimate heir. Johnson also suspected that Bobby held this view himself.

As the 1960s began, Robert Kennedy was not the liberal dove who would oppose the war in Vietnam in 1968. He was much more conservative and hawkish. He had worked for and attended the funeral of Senator Joseph McCarthy. In the entrance hall of his home at Hickory Hill, two photographs were prominently displayed. They were of the former Republican president Herbert Hoover and the Führer's favorite pope, Pius XII, who had taken an accommodating view of Fascism in Europe during the 1930s and 1940s.

After the failure of the invasion at the Bay of Pigs, Bobby was infamous within Washington's inner circles for his obsession with getting rid of Fidel Castro by any means, including assassination. During the Cuban Missile Crisis, however, Bobby showed a more dovish side, opposing those who advocated an air attack on the missile sites.

Still, the resolution of the crisis, with the Soviets withdrawing their missiles, seemed a triumph of American toughness and was so reported to the public. The most widely publicized quote from an American official was supplied by Secretary of State Dean Rusk: "We're eyeball to eyeball and the other fellow just blinked."

The Kennedys kept secret the single most dovish act in the American negotiations to resolve the crisis, when Bobby promised the Soviet ambassador, Anatoly Dobrynin, that the United States would withdraw its missiles from Turkey, a commitment that in fact McNamara carried out a few months later. John Kennedy not only concealed the truth about his dovishness from the American people but peddled disinformation to his friends Charles Bartlett and Stewart Alsop, which they published in the *Saturday Evening Post* in November 1962, saying that the president had been disturbed by Adlai Stevenson's weakness in suggesting exactly what Kennedy had secretly done—namely, offering to remove our missiles from Turkey if Russia removed its missiles from Cuba.

Bobby's chat with Dobrynin was known by only six people. It was regarded as so secret and possibly dangerous to the Kennedy reputation that, even though Robert Kennedy disclosed it

in a book not published until after his death in 1968, the book's
editor, Ted Sorensen, felt it necessary to water down the story,
making it vague and undramatic. There is no evidence that
Johnson himself knew of the episode. Robert McNamara, who
did know—and as secretary of defense would seem to have
been most likely, if not duty-bound, to tell Kennedy's successor
as commander in chief—never told Johnson about it.

Perhaps the most ironic part of this story is that during the
EXCOMM meetings, before Johnson concluded with his hawkish "cut off the head of the rattlesnake" statement, he had
argued that the United States should give up its missiles in Turkey in exchange for Russians removing theirs from Cuba, which
is of course what the Kennedy brothers and McNamara ultimately did. It is difficult to resist speculating about what course
Johnson would have followed in Vietnam if he had known that
his dovish side had been right in the missile crisis. But the fact
seems to be that he, like the American people, did not know.

So Johnson had reason to fear a hawkish Robert Kennedy in
1964. He also remembered how John Kennedy had outtoughed
Nixon in their discussions about standing up to the Communists in the 1960 presidential debates. Johnson concluded that
he had to make sure he seemed as hawkish as he thought the
Kennedys were. Johnson especially feared opposition from
Robert Kennedy at this time in late July because he had just
told Kennedy on July 29 that he was not to be Johnson's choice
for vice president in 1964. Johnson knew that the decision
angered Kennedy, and he feared that Kennedy might try to
stampede the coming Democratic convention against him.

A memorial movie about John Kennedy was to be shown at
the convention, and Johnson worried that it might set off a pro-
Bobby demonstration that would get out of control. He had seen
that very thing come close to happening at the 1960 convention,

when Adlai Stevenson walked onto the floor on Tuesday afternoon and inspired a tremendous demonstration. Delegates who
were pro-Kennedy or pro-Johnson were reminded of their
loyalty to the candidate who had been their standard-bearer in
1952 and 1956. Their cheers were deafening. Kennedy strate-
gists Ken O'Donnell and Larry O'Brien worried about what
could happen if that demonstration got out of hand. They were
saved by Stevenson himself, who deflated the demonstration
with a five-minute speech that was notably dull and uninspiring.

This time, Johnson feared, there was much more pro-
Kennedy emotion in the party than there had been for Stevenson four years earlier. Any spark could ignite it. So Johnson
definitely did not want to give Bobby the excuse to take him
on about Vietnam. His anxieties were likely stoked further by
an early August cable from General Maxwell Taylor, for whom
Bobby had named one of his sons, saying that a failure to
respond to the North Vietnamese attack on the U.S. destroyers
would be a signal "that the U.S. flinches from direct confrontation with the North Vietnamese." Nor could he have been comforted by a statement by Douglas Dillon, the Kennedy-appointed
secretary of the Treasury, for whom another of Bobby Kennedy's sons was named, who had said in an August cabinet meeting, "There is a limit on the number of times we can be attacked
by the North Vietnamese without hitting their naval bases."

So it was fear of criticism from Kennedy or Goldwater or
both that made it imperative to Johnson that he appear tough.
To demonstrate his resolve, he ordered an immediate retalia-
tory attack against North Vietnam and asked Congress to adopt
what came to be called the Tonkin Gulf Resolution, which
authorized the president "to take all necessary measures to
repel" and counter attacks on the armed forces of the United
States and to defend the freedom of South Vietnam.

And he decided to lie. On August 4, in a speech to the nation about the Tonkin Gulf incident, Johnson said, "The attacks were unprovoked."

One wonders, however, if the resolution—with the dismaying authority it gave the president—would have been passed or even proposed had Johnson and the American public known about Robert Kennedy's chat with Dobrynin two years earlier, which in effect acknowledged that our missiles in Turkey were a provocation that helped explain why the Soviet Union put missiles in Cuba, just ninety miles from Florida. If the Kennedys had revealed the American provocation in Turkey, Johnson would have had no reason to fear that Bobby would criticize him for revealing South Vietnam's provocation.

Still, the fear of Goldwater alone might have been enough to convince Johnson he had to lie. Judging by his conversation with Robert Anderson and the one that followed with Robert McNamara, Johnson began to think of downplaying the South Vietnamese provocation only after Anderson warned him about the danger of criticism from Goldwater.

And if the South Vietnamese provocation had been revealed to the public, it is likely that there would have been much less widespread support for the Tonkin Gulf Resolution. As it was, the measure gave Johnson everything he wanted; he described it as being "like grandma's nightshirt—it covered everything."

The resolution was given additional impetus by an apparent second North Vietnamese attack on the *Maddox*, and another destroyer, the *Turner Joy*, on the night of August 3. By the afternoon of the fourth, however, doubt was growing as to whether that attack had actually happened. The commander of the *Maddox* said that "freak weather effects on radar and overeager sonarmen" might have produced false evidence of torpedoes. Johnson himself later confided to George Ball, the undersecretary of state, "Hell, those dumb, stupid sailors were just shooting at flying fish!"

But on the evening of August 4, Johnson was convinced that he needed to use the incident to show the American people that he was just as tough as Goldwater or Kennedy. So in his speech to the nation that night, he not only failed to mention the provocation from the South Vietnamese but neglected to tell the American people that the second attack, on the *Maddox* and the *Turner Joy*, may not have happened at all. The Tonkin Gulf Resolution passed Congress three days later, unanimously in the House and with only two senators dissenting.

McNamara exulted to Johnson that they had "a blank-check authorization for further action."

With the Tonkin Gulf crisis behind him, Johnson turned his attention back to the 1964 presidential election. The Democratic National Convention was scheduled to take place later in August in Atlantic City, New Jersey. Everyone agreed that Johnson would be the Democratic Party's nominee. The only question was who would he choose as his vice president.

Polls of Democratic voters showed Bobby Kennedy not only leading any potential rivals but 15 percent ahead of his closest competitor. Kennedy dithered but finally decided he wanted the job. Johnson, of course, did not want Kennedy. But he too dithered. In Johnson's case, the uncertainty involved how to handle the situation.

He did not want to alienate Kennedy supporters, so he thrashed about searching for an inoffensive way of dumping him. Finally, Johnson decided to make this announcement: "I've reached the conclusion that it would be inadvisable for me to recommend to the convention any member of the cabinet or any of those who meet regularly with the cabinet."

Unfortunately, this ploy proved to be obvious to everyone,

including Bobby. In a telegram to McNamara, Rusk, Stevenson, and Shriver, Kennedy joked, "Sorry I took so many of you nice fellows over the side with me."

As for his choice among the remaining candidates, Johnson milked the suspense of its last drop of drama by delaying his decision until the last possible moment and then making Hubert Humphrey (the most obvious choice) nervous by letting reporters know he might choose Senator Thomas Dodd of Connecticut instead.

Johnson had a reason for keeping Humphrey on edge. The prospect of harmony at the convention was threatened by a challenge to the legitimacy of the all-white Mississippi delegation by a largely black group called the Mississippi Freedom Democratic Party, which had been founded as an alternative to the segregationist domination of the regular Mississippi Democrats that had prevailed since Reconstruction.

Johnson needed Humphrey to use his liberal connections to restrain the Mississippi blacks and keep them from disrupting the convention. Disruption seemed likely as the Mississippi Freedom Democratic Party demanded that its delegates be seated at the convention instead of the all-white group of party regulars. John Connally told Johnson, "If you seat those black jigaboos, the whole South will walk out."

But after an eloquent speech by the MFDP's Fannie Lou Hamer, who had been jailed and beaten for trying to vote, the credentials committee was torn between those who wanted to seat the regulars and those who were outraged by Mississippi's treatment of blacks. A subcommittee headed by Humphrey's friend Walter Mondale came up with a solution: seat the white delegates—who would agree to sign an oath to support the convention's nominee—plus two of the MFDP delegates. The white delegates, however, refused to go along and left Atlantic City in a huff. Twenty-one of the MFDP delegates, although not officially recognized by the convention, took their seats on the floor.

Johnson had been disturbed by the fight between Mississippi whites and blacks. He even hinted he would withdraw his candidacy, telling George Reedy, "I am absolutely positive that I cannot lead the South and the North." But the moment Humphrey informed him of Mondale's compromise solution, and before finding that it had been less than completely successful, Johnson seized the excuse to end his posturing, stopped talking about withdrawing, announced his choice of Humphrey as his running mate, and took off for Atlantic City in the White House helicopter.

And it should be said that the Mondale-Humphrey compromise did have one desirable effect on the convention. Even though the white Mississippi delegates left, the rest of the South stayed. Johnson won the nomination by unanimous vote, and Humphrey, of course, received the vice presidential nomination.

The convention ended as a triumph for Johnson, who was serenaded by Broadway's Carol Channing singing "Hello, Lyndon" to the title tune of her hit show *Hello, Dolly!* The only fly in the president's ointment was a twenty-two-minute ovation the delegates gave Robert Kennedy, who made a moving speech about his late brother. But it came on the final night, too late to ignite the Kennedy takeover of the convention that Johnson had feared.

And any fear that Johnson might lose the general election to Barry Goldwater quickly disappeared as polls came out in September showing the president far ahead. Gallup had him leading by 69 percent to 31 percent. Johnson's popularity caused other Democrats to turn to him for help. Among them was Bobby Kennedy himself, who had decided to run for the U.S. Senate in New York after his vice presidential disappointment.

Kennedy now found himself locked in a close race with the popular Republican incumbent Kenneth Keating.

Johnson, delighted to find Kennedy needing him instead of the other way around, responded to pleas from Bobby's aides by coming to his rescue. He made several trips to New York, telling voters, "You don't often find a man who has the heart and soul and the compassion that Bobby Kennedy has." During a joint campaign through upstate New York, a grateful Kennedy hailed Johnson as "already one of the great presidents of the United States."

Johnson was fortunate in having Goldwater as an opponent. The potential Republican candidate in 1964 that he and John Kennedy had most feared was Nelson Rockefeller, the popular governor of New York. But Rockefeller had begun to lose ground when he divorced his wife of thirty years and married a much younger woman. Still, he seemed to have recovered by the spring of 1964 and was leading in the polls to win the California primary. Then his young wife delivered a baby on the eve of the primary and what had been a comfortable lead in the polls vanished overnight.

If historians want to find a last clear moment before the sexual revolution of the 1960s took hold, it may well have been when Rockefeller's new baby arrived, reminding voters of his divorce and remarriage to a young woman. Morality was still conventional enough to cause them to abandon Rockefeller, turning what seemed like a certain victory into a crushing defeat.

With the moderate Rockefeller out of the picture, Johnson was able to seize the middle ground against Goldwater, who had left the middle wide open with his acceptance speech at the Republican Convention, where he declared, "Extremism in defense of liberty is no vice." Goldwater campaigned as if determined to lose, even denouncing Social Security. His insistence on confrontation with the Soviet Union and China accompanied by a brandishing of the bomb aroused fear among voters that he was reckless. His campaign slogan, "In your heart, you know he's right," was transformed by humorists into, "In your gut, you know he's nuts."

To guard against the most realistic of Johnson's fears, that he would lose the South, a campaign train trip from Washington to New Orleans was organized by Lady Bird. Dubbed the "Lady Bird Special," it traveled 1,628 miles through eight southern states. She knew how to appeal to the good side of southerners. "Robert E. Lee counseled us well," said her husband, summarizing his wife's message at the end of her trip, "when he told us to cast off our animosities and raise our sons to be Americans." Except for a couple of hostile crowds in South Carolina, she won over most of her usually large audiences with her own southern charm. In the end, Johnson did lose five states in the old Confederacy, but he held on to six.

With his speech about the Tonkin Gulf incident and the accompanying resolution, Johnson was able to quiet the concerns that the Republicans sought to arouse about whether he would be tough enough with the Communists.

One problem Johnson could not anticipate cropped up in October. Walter Jenkins, an able and devoted aide, was arrested for indecent behavior in the men's room of the YMCA. He had attended a cocktail party at *Newsweek*'s Washington bureau and, apparently under the influence of alcohol, had gone to the men's room of the Y a block or so away. The event occurred on October 7 but did not threaten to become public knowledge until a *Washington Star* reporter noticed the arrest on police records.

The reporter called the White House and was told that

Jenkins would call back. Instead, Jenkins called Clark Clifford and Abe Fortas, asking them to intercede on his behalf. They were by far the two heaviest hitters in Johnson's network of friendly lawyers. The regard in which they were held in Washington at the time was sufficiently high for them to succeed in persuading the editors of Washington's three major papers, the *Post*, the *Star*, and the *Daily News*, to sit on the story. But when reporters found evidence of previous similar conduct by Jenkins, the story hit the front pages.

Now panic enveloped the Johnson campaign that feared where fallout from the scandal might lead. If sexual morality became an issue, Johnson's own affairs might be considered fair game by reporters, many of whom were well aware of his indiscretions. But Johnson's luck held. Even though many in the media personally disliked Johnson, they were unusually united in preferring him over Goldwater. So they gave him a pass this time. Johnson was also comforted by a search of Pentagon files that yielded a glowing fitness report about Jenkins when he served in the air force reserve. It was signed by his commanding officer, who just happened to be one Barry Goldwater.

Jenkins resigned. Other news—China exploded an H-bomb, Nikita Khrushchev was ousted from the Soviet premiership—took over the front pages. Major scandal had been avoided. Breathing easier, the campaign moved on to triumph.

On election day, Johnson lost only those five southern states and Arizona. His popular vote margin eclipsed the record set by Franklin Roosevelt in 1936—he won by 15 million votes compared to FDR's 9 million. One result that must have been especially pleasing to Johnson: he carried New York by 2.5 million votes compared to Bobby Kennedy's margin of 719,000 in the Senate race. Democratic majorities in the House and Senate grew significantly, with the Democrats now controlling the House 295–140 and the Senate 68–32. It was a glorious victory for Johnson, giving him both the proof of public approval and the congressional majorities needed to take dramatic new strides toward what he would come to call the Great Society.

7

The Great Society

It may have been hard to take Johnson's ideas for the Great Society seriously when he first sketched them out to Dick Goodwin and Bill Moyers in the White House swimming pool in February 1964. The sight of Johnson's large body in the water made Goodwin think of Moby Dick and Moyers of a polar bear. Now, however, with the War on Poverty and the Civil Rights Act of 1964 on the books and already being implemented, those grand ideas were becoming increasingly credible. And more, much more, was soon to come.

Johnson made federal aid to education his first priority in 1965. Determined to help poor students like those he had gone to school with in the hill country and had taught in Cotulla, he knew that he had to overcome Congress's long-standing bias in favor of local control of elementary and secondary schools.

One reason for the opposition to the federal role had been a desire on the part of southern conservatives to preserve segregated schools. That factor had, however, been minimized by *Brown v. Board of Education* and the Civil Rights Act of 1964, which gave the attorney general of the United States the power to enforce the school desegregation called for by the Supreme Court.

Another stumbling block in the path of federal aid was religion. Catholic legislators from urban areas opposed any bill that did not include parochial schools, while Protestants from the rest of the country tended to be against any measure that helped such institutions. The Johnson administration decided to get around this obstacle by granting aid to students rather than to schools. This model had been accepted by Congress and the public in the case of the GI Bill, which had given World War II veterans allowances to cover their expenses whether they attended Ohio State or Notre Dame.

In *Everson v. Board of Education*, the Supreme Court had upheld this model as it applied to state aid for public and private elementary and secondary students in New Jersey. The GI Bill argument found a receptive audience on Capitol Hill, aided by the remarkable decline in anti-Catholicism that had occurred in the country since 1960, when it had been a formidable obstacle to John Kennedy's nomination and election. The fact that Kennedy had never shown any evidence of being under the sway of the Vatican, and that the late president now enjoyed such enormous posthumous popularity, helped, as did the worldwide affection for the benign Pope John XXIII.

As a result, the bill passed the House and Senate by wide margins. In the Senate, the vote was an incredible 73–18. What made this margin so remarkable was the previous failure of similar measures to attract even the barest majority.

Johnson signed the bill in front of the one-room school that he attended as a boy, with his first-grade teacher, Katie Deadrich Looney, in attendance, along with some of Johnson's pupils from Cotulla. Texas barbecue was served. A "corny, warm setting," is the way Lady Bird described it in her diary. "I will never do anything in my entire life, now or in the future," said Johnson, "that excites me more . . . or makes the land and all of its people better and wiser and stronger or anything that I think means more to freedom and justice in the world, than what we have done with this education bill."

Another education bill that was passed in 1965, the Higher Education Act, encouraged community service by students and provided aid for librarians and black colleges and, most significantly, funding for scholarships, loans, and work-study assistance that together constituted the first major federal effort to encourage young people to attend college since the GI Bill. Baby boomers had only just begun to graduate from high school, and their escalating number would make the potential impact of this bill immense.

The importance of these education bills notwithstanding, the undeniable centerpieces of Johnson's 1965 legislative program were Medicare and the Voting Rights Act.

Johnson began making the case for Medicare in two messages to Congress in early 1965. He pointed out that "four out of five persons 65 or older have a disability or chronic disease" and that "almost half of the elderly have no health insurance at all." Harry Truman had been the first president to advocate federal involvement in health care, but for two decades it had foundered on the shoals of the American Medical Association (AMA) and conservative Republicans such as the movie actor turned conservative leader Ronald Reagan, who believed that programs like Medicare would "invade every area of freedom in this country."

In addition to the physicians and the Republican right wing, Johnson had to deal with the danger that a powerful Democrat, Wilbur Mills, chairman of the House Ways and Means Committee, would oppose Medicare. Mills feared, not unreasonably, that the bill would result in large budget deficits.

But Mills, who is mostly remembered in Washington for his involvement in the 1970s with a well-endowed stripper named Fanne Foxe, was a shrewd realist. Like Everett Dirksen in the case of civil rights, Mills saw the handwriting on the wall in Johnson's landslide victory with all the liberal congressmen carried in on the president's coattails. He knew that some kind of bill was inevitable and declared that he and the Ways and Means Committee "would be able to work something out."

Mills came up with a proposal that Johnson liked: provide hospital insurance under Social Security, voluntary insurance for doctors' bills, and medical care for the poor under a state-administered program to be called Medicaid. When he presented the bill to the House, he received a standing ovation from his colleagues, who proceeded to pass it by an overwhelming margin of 313 to 115.

Two remaining obstacles now confronted Johnson. One was the AMA, which could still sabotage the bill's implementation. The other was Harry Byrd, the very conservative senior senator from Virginia, through whose Finance Committee the bill would have to pass in order to reach the Senate floor. Johnson took care of Byrd first. The morning after Medicare passed the House, Johnson invited Byrd, Mills, and other congressional leaders to the White House to discuss it. Johnson also arranged to have television cameras present. After thanking Mills for his role, Johnson turned to Byrd and asked him if he would "arrange for prompt hearings" when the bill came to the Senate. Cornered, Byrd said yes. Without the cameras, the outcome might well have been different. Byrd might have used his not inconsiderable power in the Senate to bottle up the bill.

Johnson used a similar tactic on the AMA. Inviting its leaders to the White House, he asked for their help in getting physicians to serve in Vietnam. When they agreed, Johnson called in reporters and praised the doctors' patriotism.

When the reporters asked if the doctors intended to support Medicare, Johnson replied, "Of course they'll support the law of the land," and turned to the leader of the AMA group, who dutifully declared, "We are after all law-abiding citizens and we have every intention of obeying the new law." In the event, most physicians were able to triumph over their country-club conservatism and embrace Medicare as they saw the fees it was bringing in and that it did nothing to disturb the fee-for-service model on which their practice was based.

As for the Voting Rights Act, its necessity had become increasingly clear after white southern officials succeeded, as liberal critics had predicted, in rendering largely ineffective the voting provisions of Johnson's 1957 civil rights bill. In 1964, with a project called Freedom Summer, civil rights organizations had made a major effort to register black voters. But they met with little success. In Alabama, only 19 percent of black voters succeeded in registering. In Mississippi, the figure was even worse, just 6 percent. In the State of the Union address in January 1965, Johnson called for Congress to get rid of "every remaining obstacle to the right and opportunity to vote." He also asked Nicholas Katzenbach, who had succeeded Robert Kennedy as attorney general, to draft a voting rights bill. But he stopped there, fearing that he would be pushing Congress too far if he asked for another civil rights bill after getting one passed in 1964.

Martin Luther King Jr. saw that he had to create public pressure to persuade Johnson to act. King decided to launch a program to register black voters in Selma, Alabama. The sheriff there, Jim Clark, promised to be an even uglier villain than Bull Connor had been in Birmingham. Describing blacks as "the lowest form of humanity" and wearing a button saying "Never," Clark equipped his deputies with electric cattle prods with which to attack demonstrators.

After Clark had begun to kindle outrage by assaulting hun-
dreds of demonstrators, including schoolchildren, Johnson told
King that he would support voting rights legislation. But when
Johnson would not be specific about the content of the bill,
King turned up the heat. He announced that he would lead a
march from Selma to the Alabama capital of Montgomery.

George Wallace, the state's governor, banned the march.
But, without King, who had been warned he might be assassi-
nated if he participated, some six hundred civil rights advocates
decided to start out anyway. They got as far as the Edmund Pet-
tus Bridge on the outskirts of Selma, where they found Clark's
deputies and state troopers blocking them.

Major John Cloud, leading the state troopers, gave the
marchers two minutes to disperse. Hosea Williams, the marchers' leader, said, "May we have a word with the Major?"

"There is no word to be had," replied Cloud, who a minute
later ordered, "Troopers advance!"

Within seconds, marchers were being beaten with clubs and
panicked by tear gas fired into their midst. Pursued back into
town by mounted troopers and ambushed by white posses along
the way, scores were seriously injured, including a future congressman, John Lewis, who suffered a fractured skull.

The only Selma hospital that accepted blacks found itself
overwhelmed with wounded. The ground at the bridge, in the
words of King's biographer Taylor Branch, was "littered with
abandoned purses, umbrellas, hats, packs, shoes, and prostrate
human forms, several with spewing gas canisters close by."
Television covered the event. Pictures of the marchers being
chased and beaten appeared on all three networks. ABC was
running a big movie that night that attracted 48 million view-
ers. All of them witnessed the shocking events in Selma when
the movie was interrupted to show what had happened
that day.

King's strategy worked. Public opinion sided with the march-ers in the aftermath of what came to be called Bloody Sunday. Johnson announced he would send a voters' rights bill to Con-gress. King, however, did not turn down the heat even then. He scheduled another march from Selma to Montgomery. This presented Johnson with another challenge: how to protect the marchers.

The thought Johnson devoted to handling this situation and indeed the enormous effort he put into getting the voting rights bill enacted suggests that King's pressure may not have been unwelcome. Indeed, Johnson may have been employing a tactic much favored by his hero Franklin Roosevelt, who frequently urged journalists and others to create a public demand for him to do exactly what he wanted to do, as when he transferred fifty destroyers to Britain before Hitler could invade it in 1940. Evi-dence that FDR's example was in LBJ's mind came when John-son told King that they were working the "in" and "out" together.

To protect the marchers, Johnson realized that his task would be far easier if he could persuade Governor Wallace to cooperate. So he invited Wallace to the White House. When Wallace arrived in the Oval Office, Johnson sat him on a low sofa with cushions that made him lean back. The effect was to increase the already considerable difference in height between the short Wallace and the tall president, who in his rocker loomed over the Alabama governor as they sat knee to knee.

When Wallace said he couldn't persuade local officials to reg-ister black voters, Johnson replied, "Don't shit me about your persuasive power, George. I saw you [on television] attacking me, George. And you know what? You were so damn persuasive that I had to turn off the set before you had me changing my mind."

Johnson appealed to Wallace's better self by showing him a picture of a state trooper kicking a black marcher, saying, "I know you're like me, not approving of brutality." The president continued in the same vein, asking Wallace not to think about the next election year, 1968, but about 1988: "You and me, we'll be dead and gone then, George. . . . Do you want a Great . . . Big . . . Marble monument that reads, 'George Wallace—He Built?' . . . Or do you want a little piece of scrawny pine board lying across that harsh, caliche soil, that reads, 'George Wallace—He Hated'?"

Johnson then led the thoroughly cowed governor into the Rose Garden, where reporters waited. Johnson told them that Wallace had agreed that blacks should be registered and marchers protected. Wallace did not demur.

Wallace, however, later notified the White House that he could not protect the marchers. This gave Johnson the excuse to nationalize the Alabama National Guard, which he supplemented with U.S. marshals and military police from the U.S. Army. The march proceeded, twenty-five thousand strong, culminating in a speech by King from the steps of the Alabama state capitol. There was no evidence of violence along the way or in Montgomery, but that night a white civil rights worker from Detroit, Viola Liuzzo, was shot and killed as she drove from Selma to Montgomery. Johnson immediately condemned the murder as having been done by the "enemies of justice who for decades have used the rope and the gun and the tar and the feathers to terrorize their neighbors" and repeated his demand that Congress act immediately on the voting rights bill.

Johnson had already spoken to a joint session of Congress, asking for the voting rights bill in one of his most eloquent addresses. "There is no Negro problem. There is no Southern problem. There is no Northern problem. There is only an American problem," he said, "because it's not just Negroes, but really it's all of us, who must overcome the crippling legacy of bigotry and injustice."

Johnson then paused and solemnly proclaimed, "And we shall overcome."

It was a thrilling moment, with most of the audience rising to its feet and cheering the president's reference to the civil rights movement's theme song "We Shall Overcome."

As Johnson left the podium, he shook the hand of Emanuel Celler, the chairman of the House Judiciary Committee, and said, "Manny, I want you to start hearings tonight." Johnson continued to apply the pressure, calling one congressman after another to make sure he would vote right. James Farmer of the Congress of Racial Equality observed that Johnson was "cracking the whip. He was cajoling, he was threatening," using "whatever tactic was required with that certain individual."

Johnson was employing all the political skills he had developed over a lifetime on behalf of a great cause. It may well have been the sublime moment of his life. The bill passed the Senate by 74–19 and the House by 333–85. Johnson signed it into law on August 6, 1965, saying it would "strike away the last major shackle" on American blacks.

And the new law was tough, not easy to evade as the 1957 act had been. To prove he meant business, Johnson sent federal officials to Mississippi. In one county alone, the number of registered blacks increased from 320 to 6,789.

Just five days after the passage of the Voting Rights Act, Johnson received what he must have regarded as an ironic reward. Roughly five thousand blacks in Los Angeles rioted, looting and burning stores in response to the possibly unjust arrest of a young black man suspected of drunk driving. William Parker, the Los Angeles police chief, implicitly blamed Johnson and civil rights advocates for the unrest, saying that rioting is inevitable when "you keep telling people they are unfairly treated." Johnson confided to his aide Joseph Califano that he feared black riots would halt any further progress in civil rights.

Still Johnson managed to strike another blow against bigotry. The legislative year ended in October with its final Great Soci-

ety bill, the Immigration Act of 1965. The long-standing preference for white northern Europeans embedded in U.S.
immigration law was replaced by an equal openness to people
of all colors. The result would change the face of America.

Once again, Johnson chose Emanuel Celler to guide the bill
through the House. His choice as Senate manager, Edward Kennedy, surprised observers who assumed that Johnson disliked all
the Kennedys. Teddy, however, was a natural politician, much
more to Johnson's taste than the passionate but often abrasive
Bobby.

Johnson displayed his personal concern for the bill by calling
Teddy to ask, "Where is my immigration bill, goddam it?" and
admonishing him that we've "got to pass it while the Southerners are down on the mat" from their voting rights defeat. Needless to say, Johnson got the bill passed. Fittingly, he signed it at
the foot of the Statue of Liberty, whose promise he was now
fulfilling.

If there was a failure of the Great Society, it was a failure to
face underlying problems. Medicare, by doing nothing to reform
the fee-for-service system, left in place a major contributor to
the ever-escalating cost and inefficient delivery of health care.
Johnson's education bill failed to confront the issue of teacher
quality, which only grew in importance as bright women found
opportunity in other professions and as too many teacher-training
institutions continued to resist improvement. In the 1960s,
however, few spoke up about these matters, and not enough
have spoken since to bring about the reforms that are needed.
If there is blame, it is far from being Lyndon Johnson's alone.
And there can be no doubt that his Great Society, whatever its
flaws, has done great good for this country.

8

Escalation

It was a couple of hours after midnight on Sunday, February 7, 1965. Most of the U.S. military advisers and helicopter pilots stationed at Pleiku in South Vietnam were asleep. Suddenly their quarters were wracked by a series of explosions, some from satchel charges planted by the Viet Cong. Others came from mortar shells raining down on the American soldiers struggling out of bed. As they emerged into the open, many who had not already been hit were picked off by Viet Cong riflemen. Bill Mauldin, the famous World War II cartoonist, who happened to be visiting his son, a helicopter pilot at Pleiku, described the scene: "Dead and dying were everywhere, and everything was covered with blood."

McGeorge "Mac" Bundy, Johnson's national security adviser, also happened to be in Vietnam. He hurried to Pleiku and was horrified by the carnage. As Robert McNamara put it, "The event shook Bundy," who called the White House and urged immediate retaliation against the Viet Cong's sponsor and ally North Vietnam. The emotion in the voice of a man McNamara described as normally a detached rationalist lent special force to his message.

Johnson convened a meeting of his national security team within ten hours of the attack. Those attending included McNamara; General Earle Wheeler, the chairman of the Joint Chiefs of Staff; CIA director John McCone; Undersecretary of State George Ball; and Senate majority leader Mike Mansfield. "We have kept our gun over the mantel . . . for a long time now," the president said, referring to the fact that the United States had not attacked the North since the Tonkin Gulf episode. "And what was the result? They are killing our men while they sleep in the night."

Feelings ran strong in the room. The United States had resisted the temptation to take the war to the North, even as the situation in the South had been deteriorating for months. The South Vietnamese army appeared to be losing, with its government in disarray. Now was the time for the United States to strike back at the North—and, at the same time, buck up its disheartened allies in the South.

Of Johnson's advisers that day, only Mike Mansfield urged restraint. All the rest, even the normally dovish George Ball, favored attacking the North. Mac Bundy was so eager to retaliate that he sped back to Washington without a rest stop to break the long journey, arriving in Washington at 11 p.m. that night. Even though badly jet-lagged, he rushed to the White House to press his case. But victory was already his. Johnson's decision to attack the North had been made.

The targets chosen were North Vietnamese barracks just across the border from South Vietnam. That bombing did not, however, deter the Viet Cong. On the night of February 10, the guerrillas struck again, this time hitting the U.S. barracks at Qui Nhon.

Johnson decided to continue bombing with a series of air strikes against the North called Rolling Thunder. This was the beginning of a policy of graduated response, designed to subject the North Vietnamese to increasing pressure until they agreed to negotiate. However, North Vietnam's largest cities—the capital, Hanoi, and its major seaport, Haiphong—where the most damage could have been inflicted, were excluded because the Johnson team feared that attacking them might bring China or the Soviet Union into the war.

This meant that Rolling Thunder's extended air raids failed to deter attacks on American bases in the South from the Viet Cong. So in late February, General William Westmoreland, the top U.S. military commander in Vietnam, requested two battalions of marines to guard the American airbase at Da Nang.

The U.S. ambassador, Maxwell Taylor, opposed Westmoreland's request. Taylor worried about how "'white-faced' soldiers" would fare in "Asian forests and jungles" as they tried to distinguish between Viet Cong and friendly Vietnamese forces. How "could [they] do much better" than the French army that had been humiliated at Dien Bien Phu in 1954—the defeat that drove France from Indochina?

But Johnson sided with Westmoreland. On March 8, the marines arrived. It was a fateful moment. For the first time, the United States had committed ground combat troops to Vietnam.

Ironically, Johnson foresaw the tragedy that would unfold. He confided to Senator Richard Russell: "I guess we've got no choice. But it scares the death out of me. [The Viet Cong] are not going to run. Then you're tied down." And, accurately predicting the Pentagon's tendency to escalate its requests, he told Senator Mike Mansfield: "If they get 150, they will have to get another 150, and then they will have to get another 150."

But those who saw trouble ahead were few. An uncritical press depicted marines being greeted by pretty Vietnamese girls with garlands of flowers.

Johnson's prediction about the military's appetite for increasing numbers of troops was borne out in mid-March when Westmoreland asked for two army divisions. What had been a need for 3,000 marines two weeks earlier had been transformed to a need to add 30,000 soldiers. The Joint Chiefs wanted to up the ante to 45,000. Again, Ambassador Taylor resisted. And he had to be taken seriously. After all, he had credentials that could not be ignored, having been the heroic commander of a World War II airborne division and a pioneer in foreseeing the need for the army to prepare to fight unconventional wars.

So Johnson asked Taylor and Westmoreland to meet with McNamara and the Joint Chiefs in Honolulu. The result was a compromise. Westmoreland would get 40,000 soldiers but, to appease Taylor, their operations were limited to within fifty miles of the bases they were to protect.

Westmoreland, moreover, won still another concession. He wanted to send combat patrols beyond the defensive perimeter, to have his troops, as one of his officers put it, "start killing the Viet Cong instead of just sitting on their ditty box." Westmoreland's argument that a good offense is the best defense persuaded Johnson to approve his proposal.

Again, the press failed to see the significance of the escalation, as in this front-page headline in the *New York Times*: "President Plans No Major Change in Vietnam Policy—Raids on North Will Continue but American Combat Role Is Still Being Avoided."

A rare exception to the media's blindness was Hanson Baldwin of the *Times*. On April 21, he wrote about "plans for a major buildup of United States ground forces," with a "passive defense" giving way to a more "active defense" and with "combat patrols well beyond the perimeter." Furthermore, Baldwin foresaw the future: "Eventually, if necessary the combat units may go over to an active offensive to help the South Vietnamese regular forces seek out and destroy Viet Cong."

The editors of the *Times* chose to place Baldwin's prophetic

piece on an inside page. To the extent that concern about escalation was expressed in the media and in the antiwar movement that was now aborning, it was almost always about the
bombing and rarely about the ground forces that would eventually be the major factor in the slaughter to come.

On April 28 a cable arrived at the White House concerning
an event on the other side of the globe that temporarily diverted
attention from the conflict in Southeast Asia. The cable came
from Ambassador W. Tapley Bennett in Santo Domingo, the
capital of the Dominican Republic. Bennett described a civil
conflict that had broken out in the country a few days earlier.
His cable warned, "Situation deteriorating rapidly," and concluded, "Country team unanimously of opinion that time has
come to land Marines."

Johnson immediately dispatched 400 marines. Then a back-
and-forth tug-of-war in Washington began between two fac-
tions of the administration. One, led by the State Department's
Thomas Mann and Jack Vaughn, expressed fear that Communists allied with Fidel Castro would assume control of the rebel
group or already dominated it. They favored major American
intervention.

"Wait a minute," counseled the other group, led by Dick
Goodwin, McGeorge Bundy, and Johnson's friend Abe Fortas.
They worried this would be the "first military intervention in
Latin America since U.S. troops left Nicaragua in the 1920s"
and would contradict the spirit of Franklin Roosevelt's Good
Neighbor Policy and John F. Kennedy's Alliance for Progress,
not to mention the charter of the Organization of American
States. They feared that once again the United States would be
charged with "Yankee imperialism."

From the beginning, Johnson seemed more sympathetic to
the side of the interventionists, declaring he was not going "to
sit here with my hands tied and let Castro take that island.

What can we do in Vietnam if we can't clean up the Dominican Republic?"

The Dominican rebels favored the return to power of Juan Bosch, a liberal non-Communist who had been elected president in December 1962 and was then overthrown by a military coup and replaced by the rich right-winger Donald Reid Cabral. Cabral proved to be unpopular, so Bosch's party, the PRD (Dominican Revolutionary Party), rose again in public favor, threatening the power of the conservative military that backed Cabral. When the conservatives tried to arrest the fellow officers who favored Bosch, the PRD encouraged the people to rise against the regime. They seized the presidential palace, whereupon the dominant military faction had air force planes attack the palace and the poor areas of Santo Domingo where Bosch's supporters were concentrated. The rebels responded by seizing Radio Santo Domingo, taking over the city center, and looting the homes of the wealthy. Americans at a hotel were briefly detained at gunpoint, prompting Ambassador Bennett to send his April 28 cable. The next day, rebel snipers fired on the embassy itself.

Johnson told Fortas that, though the rebellion had "started out as a Bosch operation," the CIA reported it had been taken over by Communists and now "is completely led, operated, dominated—they've got men on the inside of it—Castro operation." It is unclear whether Johnson was totally accurate in describing the CIA's reporting, but there is no question that the FBI's J. Edgar Hoover was supplying Johnson with report after report of Communist infiltration of the rebel cause.

Reports from Ambassador Bennett took on a tone of panic and then became further exaggerated by Johnson, who told the public: "Some 1500 innocent people were murdered and shot, and their heads cut off, and six Latin American embassies were violated and fired upon over a period of four days before we went in. As we talked to our ambassador to confirm the horrors and the tragedy and the unbelievable fact that they were firing on Americans and the American embassy, he was talking to us from under a desk while bullets were going through his windows."

None of these "facts" found confirmation from independent reporters on the scene, but Johnson was determined not to let his conservative critics accuse him of "losing Cuba again" in the Dominican Republic. He ordered a major intervention. By May 17 the United States had put 22,000 troops into the Dominican Republic.

Fortunately for Johnson, his diplomats (with the aid of the Organization of American States) organized a truce in May. Johnson, realizing that his actions in the Dominican Republic were getting him into trouble with American liberals, then persuaded Rómulo Betancourt of Venezuela and José Figueres Ferrer of Costa Rica, two former Latin American presidents who were highly regarded by liberals in the United States, to help broker a more permanent reconciliation in August, leading to a provisional government in Santo Domingo and an election the following June. In that election Bosch was defeated by Joaquín Balaguer, whose conservatism was not of the extreme nature that had produced the rebellion in the first place.

These developments gradually removed the Dominican Republic from American front pages. But during the spring of 1965, the crisis there succeeded in at least temporarily diverting the minds of liberal critics from Vietnam. Thus, when the historian Arthur Schlesinger Jr. spoke at a teach-in in Washington that had been intended to focus on Vietnam, he attacked America's bombing of the North but failed to make any mention of the ground war, while devoting most of his time to criticizing Johnson's actions in the Dominican Republic.

Meanwhile, across the world, the Viet Cong and the North

Vietnamese launched a series of attacks in May that left the South's army badly battered. By early June its disintegration seemed imminent. Westmoreland asked for still more ground troops, a lot more.

Because of the threatened collapse of South Vietnam, American troops became increasingly active, as Hanson Baldwin had anticipated, with their "defense" taking on an aggressive character. Westmoreland now favored abandoning Taylor's enclave strategy in favor of the search-and-destroy policy Baldwin had predicted.

Critics of the war, however, continued to ignore the ground war and focus on the bombing. Though still a minority, their number was growing. Led by the newspaper columnists Walter Lippmann and Joseph Kraft, and by Senators Frank Church, George McGovern, and William Fulbright, the antiwar movement attracted twenty thousand to an April demonstration in Washington and thousands more to teach-ins at universities, like the one at which Arthur Schlesinger spoke. But Johnson retained the support of the public as a whole, with 70 percent approval ratings for his Vietnam policy.

Within the administration, only George Ball warned against the escalation of the ground war. Among the Republicans in Congress, only Representatives Gerald Ford and Melvin Laird expressed concern about the expansion of U.S. ground forces in Vietnam. So it is not surprising that Robert McNamara encountered little opposition when he requested 200,000 more troops for Westmoreland by the end of 1965. Although approval seemed certain, Johnson made sure that the request received thorough discussion at a series of meetings with top officials at the White House from July 21 to July 27. He realized that the decision reached would be momentous, for if the Westmoreland request were granted, it would mean turning a war that had been conducted by South Vietnam with American help into one conducted

by Americans with South Vietnamese assistance. Johnson began
the meetings by asking: "What I would like to know is what has
happened in recent months that requires this kind of decision
on my part? What are the alternatives? I want this discussed in
full detail from everyone around the table."

Although all but two of the people participating in the meetings over the next six days approved of McNamara's proposal,
concerns were expressed during the discussions that deserved
more attention than they received at the time.

One worry concerned the ineptitude of the South Vietnamese government led by General Nguyen Cao Ky—who adorned
himself with a white scarf and twin pearl-handled revolvers—
which was the product of the most recent of a series of coups
that had followed the murder of Diem in 1963. Carl Rowan, the
head of the United States Information Agency, said, "What
bothers me most is the weakness of the [South Vietnamese]
government."

McNamara added, "Ky will fall soon. He is weak."

And Johnson chimed in, "I don't see how you can fight a war
under the direction of people whose government changes every
month."

Ambassador Henry Cabot Lodge concluded, "I don't think
we ought to take this government seriously."

Although there was little explicit dissent from these harsh
judgments, the conferees consciously or unconsciously seemed
to decide to bury their concerns or simply to ignore Ky and his
government in their plan. Similarly, when Johnson asked, "Can
Westerners in the absence of accurate intelligence successfully
fight Asians in the jungle rice paddies?" and the same concern
was expressed by George Ball, no reassuring reply was forth-
coming. The group seemed to conclude without explicitly saying
so that the answer to Johnson's question was yes, we can fight in
Asian rice paddies and jungles without accurate intelligence.

And when Johnson specifically asked, "Are we getting good intelligence out of the North," he could hardly have been comforted by McNamara's reply: "Only reconnaissance and tactical soundings. We have none from combat intelligence." At one point all the doubts seemed to be getting to Johnson. "If you've made a commitment to jump off a building and you find out how high it is, you may withdraw that commitment," he said.

Whatever temptation Johnson may have felt not to jump must have been exacerbated when Bundy, playing devil's advocate, summarized the arguments against McNamara's proposal to escalate the ground war: "The argument we will face is, one, for 10 years every step we have taken has been based on a previous failure. All we have done is failed and that caused us to take another step which failed. As we go further into the fog we get deeply bruised. Also we have made excessive claims we haven't been able to realize. Two, also after 20 years of warning about war in Asia we are now doing what MacArthur and others have warned us about. We are about to fight a war we can't fight and win as the country we are trying to help is quitting. Three, there is a failure on our own to fully realize what guerrilla war is like. We are content with sending conventional troops to do an unconventional job. Four: How long? How much? Can we take casualties over five years—aren't we talking about a military solution when the solution is really political? Why can't we interdict there? Why are our bombings so fruitless? Why can't we blockade the coast? Why can't we improve our intelligence? Why can't we find the Viet Cong?"

The only reply to Bundy's seemingly devastating case came from McNamara, who said, "I think we can answer most of the questions posed."

But no one asked McNamara what those answers were or about which questions he couldn't answer. And, incredibly, Bundy dismissed his own arguments, saying, "Let us sum up—the world, the country, and the Vietnamese people would have an alarming reaction if we got out."

Secretary of State Dean Rusk added another point that seemed to influence the group. "If the Communist world finds out we will not pursue our commitments to the end," he said, "I don't know what will stay their hand."

McNamara then itemized how the "domino effect" meant that the loss of Vietnam would lead to losses elsewhere: "Laos, Cambodia, Thailand, Burma—the ripple effect will be great in China and India. We will have to give up some bases. Ayub [Khan, the leader of Pakistan] would move closer to China. Greece, Turkey [would] move to neutralist position. Communist agitation will increase in Africa."

The final nail in the coffin of the anti-escalation cause came from Admiral David McDonald, the chief of naval operations. "By putting in more men, it will turn the tide," he predicted. "Sooner or later we will force [the North Vietnamese] to the conference table."

It is worth noting that Johnson himself raised the most doubts about escalation. Did he do this for the record, or were his doubts real? Evidence for the suspicion that the former is the case is supplied by this concern Johnson expressed during the deliberations: "Remember they're going to write stories about this like they wrote about the Bay of Pigs. Stories about me and my advisers."

Whether for the record or out of sincere concern, Johnson behaved with courtesy and solicitude toward the only outright opponents of the escalation, George Ball and Senator Mike Mansfield, making sure they had ample opportunity to express their doubts.

Ball's case was this: "We cannot win, Mr. President. The war will be long and protracted. The most we can hope for is a messy conclusion. If the war is long and protracted as I believe it will be, then we will suffer because the world's greatest power cannot defeat guerrillas. . . . The enemy cannot even be seen in Vietnam. He is indigenous to the country. I truly have serious doubts that an army of Westerners can successfully fight Orientals in the Asian jungle. I think a long, protracted war will disclose our weaknesses, not our strength. . . . Take our losses, let this [South Vietnamese] government fall apart, negotiate, discuss, knowing full well there will probably be a takeover by the Communists."

Mansfield argued a similar case: "Whatever pledge we had was to assist South Vietnam in its own defense. There has been no government of legitimacy, we owe this government nothing. No redemption of any pledge of any kind. We are going deeper into war. Even total victory would be vastly costly. Our best hope we have is a quick stalemate and negotiations. We cannot expect our people to support a war for 3–5 years. What we are about to get is an anti-Communist crusade on and on. Remember, escalation begets escalation."

But with Mansfield and Ball having been the only dissenters, the president made a decision that he announced on July 28: "I have today ordered to Vietnam the air mobile division and certain other forces which will raise our fighting strength from 75,000 to 125,000 men almost immediately. Additional forces will be needed later and they will be sent as requested." These last words meant there was no limit on the number of troops that could be sent, making endless escalation possible.

Not calling up the reserves represented the only concession given to the doves. Otherwise, the July 21–27 meetings represented a total triumph for the hawks. Curiously enough, those attending the final meeting on July 27 included two men thought to have been doves, Richard Goodwin and Bill Moyers.

Why didn't the doves speak up? One reason was that they were concentrating their antiwar effort on the bombing—Johnson called Moyers "Mr. Stop the Bombing." And the combination of Johnson's domineering personality and peer pressure from the group's hawkish majority tended to discourage dissent. Chester Cooper, a member of Johnson's national security staff who was not present at the July 27 meeting but did attend several similar sessions, recalled: "I would frequently fall into a Walter Mitty–like fantasy, when my turn came I would rise to my feet and say very quietly and emphatically, 'Mr. President, I most definitely do not agree!' But I was removed from my fantasy when I heard the president calling me, and I answered, 'I agree.' "

Johnson's announcement of the decision to escalate concluded with these words: "I have spoken of divisions, but I know them all. I have seen them on the thousand streets and a hundred towns in every state of the union, working and laughing and building, and filled with hope and life. I think I know how their mothers weep and their families sorrow."

Trapped by what he thought he had to do, Johnson continued to see clearly where all this was heading. Lady Bird overheard him saying: "I don't want to get in a war and I don't see any way out of it. I've got to call up 600,000 boys, make them leave their homes and families."

The *New York Times*'s account of the July 28 press conference ran under the headline "President's Wife Is Near Tears." It was not hard to believe that Lady Bird was near tears because no one understood better than she that her husband was haunted by the possibility that each step he was taking could lead to a tragic end. She had begun to notice troubling symptoms in the president and asked two friends who were physicians to examine him. They reported he was laboring under "this heavy load of tension and this fog of depression."

Moyers described Johnson as "tormented" as he foresaw that the record of his presidency would be ruined by Vietnam. And Johnson himself, a man not ordinarily given to introspection, wrote about being "sleepless at night" and of his "lonely vigils." And he spoke publicly of the decision to send young men to die as "the most agonizing and the most painful duty of your president."

Why then did Johnson decide to escalate the war by committing American combat troops to battle? Why would he risk spoiling the incredible record of domestic accomplishment that he was making at that very moment? His Elementary and Secondary Education Act passed on April 9, Medicare on July 9, and, on perhaps the greatest day of his life, at least in terms of its triumph over two hundred years of racial prejudice, he signed the Voting Rights Act on August 6. These historic measures are mentioned again only to emphasize the stark contrast between Johnson's domestic record and the looming disaster in Vietnam.

A cynical explanation of Johnson's decisions to escalate— and cynicism is seldom without a role in understanding the tangle of motives that lay behind Johnson's actions—is that he thought he just might get away with it without too much political damage.

He constantly tried to downplay the significance of the escalation. As the war went on, he concealed the true financial cost from the public, and the increases in troop strength were usually minimized. When he announced the increase at the press conference on July 28, he neglected to mention the total number of troops he had agreed to deploy. Nor did he use General Westmoreland's term "search and destroy" to describe their new mission, which he had also approved. When he spoke to the nation about the increase, he chose a time of day when the audience would be at a minimum, rather than a time in the evening, when he would draw the largest audience.

One other reason he thought he might get away with the troop escalation was the kind of military draft in place in 1965. It offered those who wanted to avoid Vietnam enough possibility of deferment—marriage, college, graduate school, service in the reserves or National Guard—that the clever or well connected (like Dick Cheney, Bill Clinton, and George W. Bush) could avoid going to Vietnam. So when Johnson doubled the draft call as he was announcing the July escalation, he knew he was not going to upset the lives of those with enough clout to turn their anger into effective political action. Although Johnson would complain to his staff about the unfairness of the draft and even appointed a commission that recommended ending the college deferment, he retained that deferment and never called up the reserves or the National Guard. Men from these groups and the parents of the college students were likely to have community roots that could make them troublesome opponents.

Still, though one suspects that comforting if cynical thoughts about the nature of the draft occasionally occurred to Johnson, a clear preponderance of the evidence indicates that his concern about the young draftees who were going to die was genuine, however misguided his actions may seem.

The torment Bill Moyers and Lady Bird described was evident to others. One day that summer of 1965, a group of Peace Corps volunteers stood in the Oval Office as Johnson turned what was supposed to be a five-minute speech into more than an hour of agonized explanation of what he was doing in Vietnam, accompanied by an emotional reading of letters from mothers who had lost their sons, to show that he understood the terrible cost of war. Others who saw him during this period had similar experiences, as brief meetings would go on and on, sometimes lasting well into the night, as Johnson tried to justify the war to them—and, one had to suspect, to himself.

The justification he would most often cite was the domino theory. Underlying this theory was the fear of another Munich, the capitulation to Nazi aggression that set the stage for World War II. Johnson and his advisers wanted history to rank them with the Winston Churchills, not the Neville Chamberlains.

This helps explain why Johnson sought and was heartened to receive former president Eisenhower's support for his Vietnam policy.

Even more of a factor was Johnson's fear of reliving the "Who lost China?" debate of the 1950s. Back then the Republicans, egged on by Henry Luce's powerful magazines *Time* and *Life*, had crucified the Democrats for allowing China to fall to the Communists in 1949, during Harry Truman's term in office. The Democrats resisted this charge. Most of them thought the Nationalist Chinese under General Chiang Kai-shek had been hopelessly corrupt, with an army distinguished only by its ineptitude.

Still, this great fear lurked in the back of the minds of Democrats in the 1960s. Even though they did not think they had lost China in the first place, they did not want to be nailed to that cross again. Here's how Johnson put it in his memoir: "A divisive debate about 'who lost Vietnam' would be, in my judgment, even more destructive to our national life than the argument over China had been."

Similar reasoning had played a part in Johnson's response to the crisis in the Dominican Republic that spring. With his fear that the Communists would end up prevailing stoked by false alarms from J. Edgar Hoover about Reds behind every tree in the Dominican forest, Johnson acted because he could not afford to lose Cuba again.

Johnson desperately wanted peace in Vietnam. He would have been delighted to accept any deal with the North Vietnamese leader Ho Chi Minh that would have left South Vietnam free to choose its own future. He frequently extended the olive branch, including several bombing halts and numerous diplomatic overtures through friendly countries, through the United Nations, and even through the Soviet Union. He made a speech at Johns Hopkins University in April that offered to create a

Tennessee Valley Authority for all Vietnam on the Mekong River. Still, the North Vietnamese refused to sit down at the table until 1968, and even thereafter, they would never agree to abandon the Viet Cong or to remove their troops from the South.

Given that he had no one to negotiate with, Johnson's only alternative was to give up. And that he could not do. Johnson had grown up in a Texas dominated by the legend of the Alamo. Davy Crockett and Jim Bowie fought to the last man rather than surrender. Johnson so identified with the legend that he even falsely claimed that one of his ancestors had died there with the other heroes.

Nothing was more important to Johnson than being seen as courageous. A presidential aide who was planning to leave the White House asked Johnson's secretary Vicky McCammon how he could make sure of receiving a warm farewell letter from the president. Vicki said, "Be sure to tell him you admire his courage." The aide followed her advice—and he got the warm letter.

So the war continued through the rest of 1965 and all of 1966. The fresh American troops brought some victories, notably in the Ia Drang Valley near Pleiku, where they killed nearly 2,000 North Vietnamese at the cost of 300 Americans. Still the Communists managed to increase their forces by more than they were losing. After a November 1965 trip to Vietnam, Robert McNamara predicted the United States would need 600,000 troops by 1968 and that even this number would "not guarantee success." He urged Johnson to halt the bombing for four weeks and seek negotiations.

George Ball, McGeorge Bundy, and Dean Rusk agreed with McNamara. But the Joint Chiefs and civilian advisers Abe Fortas and Clark Clifford dissented, contending that a bombing halt would be a sign of weakness. Johnson came down on the side of the doves, and a thirty-seven-day bombing halt ensued. Top diplomats such as Averell Harriman were dispatched to more than forty nations to urge other countries to support negotiations, which Johnson offered without "precondition." Hanoi, however, dismissed the American effort as a trick, and as January 1966 came to a close, Johnson decided to resume bombing.

Resumption of the bombing may have sabotaged a genuine opportunity for negotiation later that year. A Polish diplomat, Janusz Lewandowski, had arranged for a meeting between American and North Vietnamese officials to be held in Warsaw. But North Vietnam became upset when American bombers struck targets near Hanoi and Haiphong. When Averell Harriman and Chester Cooper urged Johnson to order another bombing pause, they were now opposed by Dean Rusk, who had favored the long bombing halt in January. Rusk had switched sides and, supported by Walt Rostow, the hawkish national security adviser who had replaced McGeorge Bundy, he persuaded Johnson to continue the bombing. North Vietnam decided not to go to Warsaw.

Rostow's reputation with the press and the public was given an initial boost by an endorsement from the *New York Times*, which said that his "appointment places beside the President an independent and cultivated mind that, as in the Bundy era, should assure comprehension both of the intricacies of world problems and the options from which the White House must choose." The *Times* may have been at least partially justified in so describing Bundy, but it was wrong about Rostow, who focused on giving the president only the facts that fit the case he wanted to make. For example, he once asked the CIA for a list of achievements in Vietnam. He was given what he requested, but the CIA also added a list of "setbacks and losses." Rostow gave the first list to the president but omitted the second.

Back home, the peace movement gained strength in 1966. When Johnson resumed bombing at the end of January, Senator

Robert Kennedy declared that the president's actions "may become the first in a series of steps on a road from which there is no turning back—a road that leads to catastrophe for all mankind." Senator William Fulbright told a lecture audience at Johns Hopkins University that the United States was manifesting the "arrogance of power," that the nation was "in danger of losing its perspective on what exactly is within the realm of its power and what is beyond it."

But when Senator Wayne Morse of Oregon tried to repeal the Tonkin Gulf Resolution, he was able to muster the support of only five of his colleagues. Perhaps the mood of the country in 1966 was best captured in the headline of an article that Neil Sheehan wrote for the *New York Times Magazine,* "Not a Dove, but No Longer a Hawk." The article told of Sheehan's disillusionment with South Vietnam's ruling class, "mandarins drawn from the merchant and landowning families," who had staffed the French colonial civil service and now incorporated "the worst of the two cultures—the pretentiousness of the native mandarins and the rigidity of the French." Though Sheehan acknowledged that genuinely decent and patriotic people were also in this group, he found that "most of the men who ruled Saigon, like the Bourbons, seek to retain the privileges they have and to regain those that they have lost."

The South Vietnamese government was notable for its corruption. American aid destined to help South Vietnam too often found itself used by officials to enrich themselves. "What gets down to the poor son of a bitch in the paddy fields," one American adviser told Sheehan, "is a trickle." Another American, a special forces captain, told the reporter what happened to rice he had flown to a camp filled with thousands of refugees: "The local district chief confiscated the rice and sold it to the refugees at enormous prices." Needless to say, such leaders had little chance of inspiring the South Vietnamese people and their army in the struggle against the Viet Cong and the North.

This is not to say that large numbers of South Vietnamese did not want to be Communists. Sheehan described a hamlet where nearly half the villagers were Viet Cong sympathizers, but the other half "were about equally divided between those with neutral attitudes or who were [South Vietnamese government] sympathizers." But since the South Vietnamese leaders lacked the ability to inspire the people to fight, Sheehan concluded, the burden of the conflict had to be borne by the Americans.

As clearly as Sheehan saw the situation, he was typical of moderate American opinion at the time, unable to free himself from the same kind of thinking that trapped Lyndon Johnson. "If the United States were to disengage from Vietnam under adverse conditions, I believe that the political and psychological shockwaves might undermine our entire position in Southeast Asia," he concluded.

9

A Cultural Revolution

During the winter of 1966–67, it became evident that Washington, along with the rest of the nation, was undergoing a cultural sea change, with a new generation rejecting old values, asserting new rights and new freedoms—and in the process upsetting its elders but also influencing them, including members of the Johnson administration.

The cultural revolution had its roots in the 1950s. The movie *Rebel Without a Cause* in 1955, Allen Ginsberg's poem *Howl* in 1956, and Jack Kerouac's novel *On the Road* in 1957 gave early warnings of a rejection of conformity that became widespread in the second half of the 1960s. The civil rights movement, which had attained prominence in the 1950s, not only swept to historic victories in the 1960s, it spawned the assertion of other rights. Women who read Helen Gurley Brown's 1962 bestseller *Sex and the Single Girl* decided that they had a right to enjoy the sexual freedom conferred by the recent introduction of the birth control pill. Betty Friedan's 1963 manifesto *The Feminine Mystique* inspired them to demand the same career fulfillment heretofore largely open only to men. By the end of the decade homosexuals would call for gay rights and organizers of the poor would claim welfare as a right.

As new rights were asserted, an old duty was denied. Young men, who from the enactment of the draft in 1940 had accepted military service as a duty, became alarmed by the daily news of death in Vietnam, in a war that struck them as far from righteous. Fear of being drafted became a major spur to the antiwar movement. The more the war was seen as unjust, the better the excuse young men had for avoiding service.

The stirrings against the old order in popular music that began in the 1950s with Elvis Presley and rock and roll became a full-scale revolt in the 1960s. Traditional musical instruments were replaced or enhanced by electronic devices. The songs of Cole Porter, Irving Berlin, Jerome Kern, and George Gershwin practically disappeared from the airwaves. Now it was the Beatles who swept the country. A louder, harsher, even more rebellious form of rock and roll, pioneered by the Rolling Stones, quickly followed. There was also a resurgence of folk music that, though it remained traditional in form, became antiestablishment in content. Singers such as Bob Dylan, Pete Seeger, and Joan Baez appealed to young people with songs like "Blowin' in the Wind," "The Times They Are a-Changin'," and "Where Have All the Flowers Gone?," which endorsed rebellion against their parents and appealed to the antiwar sentiment now almost universal among educated youth.

Because folk songs did not raise the volume to the earsplitting level of most of the new music, it was easier for those over thirty to take and thus more influential in their attitude. One could, for example, see administration officials at folk concerts in Washington in the second half of the 1960s. But even when they did not attend such events or otherwise participate in the cultural revolution, it had tremendous impact on their lives.

Consider the experience of one administration member, ficti-
tious but close to what happened to many.

Imagine this hardworking official arriving home at night
around 9:00 p.m., looking forward to being presented with his
slippers and a nice cold martini by a wife filled with admiration
for his dedicated public service. But beginning in 1965 and
increasingly thereafter, he is met by a wife who complains about
being stuck with all the housework, asking why she can't have a
career, and, by the way, why doesn't he make love to her more
often.

She reports that their twenty-year-old son has left his dorm
at Columbia University and moved to the Lower East Side so he
can join its growing community of hippies and be near his
idol Allen Ginsberg. This is the same son who last Christmas
announced he was gay and could no longer bear the hypocrisy
of the closet. His eighteen-year-old sister, in her last year at the
National Cathedral School, comes downstairs for dinner and
asks her father why he doesn't have the guts to come out against
the war. Humiliated and angered by her attack, the official pro-
ceeds to take on his daughter's sex life, berating her for sleeping
around even before she's graduated from high school, and also
complaining about the loud music coming from her room,
which he says is destroying his hearing.

Probably no official in the Johnson administration had it that
bad, but enough of the story did happen to many to leave them
shaken. Their wives were not who they thought they were. Nor
were their children. And they were beginning to suspect that
the war was not what they had thought it was, either.

One of the rebellious families belonged to Robert McNamara, whose son, Craig, and daughter Kathleen opposed the
war. Kathleen invited antiwar activists like Sam Brown into the
McNamara home, and the secretary of defense found himself
questioning the war more and more.

McNamara also felt pressure from his aide John McNaughton, who had begun having his own doubts. By early in 1966, McNamara was telling reporters off the record that the bombing of North Vietnam was not working. During the summer, he commissioned a group of academics to perform what became known as the Jason study. It found that North Vietnam was "basically a subsistence agricultural economy" that could not be seriously damaged by bombing, that instead the bombing "clearly strengthened popular support of the [North Vietnamese] regime by engendering patriotic and nationalistic enthusiasm to resist the attacks" by the Americans.

By the fall McNamara saw "no reasonable way to bring the war to an end soon." He began to think of ways not to win the war but simply to hold on to the status quo. He proposed building an electronic fence across the border between North and South, an idea that proved unworkable but was nonetheless revealing about McNamara's state of mind.

His new attitude enraged the Joint Chiefs of Staff, who sought whatever escalation might be needed to bring victory. Refereeing the conflict between McNamara and the Joint Chiefs absorbed much of Johnson's time during the fall of 1966 and all of 1967.

Johnson's hawkish side displayed itself during a visit in October 1966 to the U.S. base at Cam Ranh Bay in South Vietnam, where he urged the troops to "nail the coonskin to the wall." Again, in his January 1967 State of the Union address, he told Congress that America would "stand firm." The hawkish Johnson continued to find reinforcement in the counsel of Walt Rostow. Rostow had a thoroughly reasonable manner that reflected his professorial background at the Massachusetts Institute of Technology (MIT). But he never wavered in his conviction that the United States could win the war, a position that usually found enthusiastic support from the Joint Chiefs and General Westmoreland.

Another increasingly influential official, Robert Komer, who was in charge of the pacification program in the South, shared Rostow's hawkishness. In support of his position, he swamped Johnson with optimistic statistics about the progress in pacification. On Capitol Hill the hawk in Johnson enjoyed firm support from Senator John Stennis and his Armed Forces Committee.

Johnson would complain that all his hawkish advisers could do was tell him to "bomb, bomb, bomb. That's all they know." But he could also ridicule the doves, calling one of their leaders, Senator William Fulbright, "Senator Halfbright." He began to suggest that McNamara's mind had been poisoned by Robert Kennedy, whose friendship with McNamara was well known. This made Johnson tend to discount McNamara's counsel as it became more dovish during 1967.

By early June 1967, however, an adviser Johnson trusted far more than he did McNamara, Harry McPherson, was confiding his own doubts in a confidential memo to the president: "It sounds romantic to say so, but if I were a young peasant, living in a hamlet, and had had none of my family hurt or killed by the Viet Cong, if I saw that the ridiculous South Vietnamese education system would almost certainly deny me the chance to go beyond the fifth grade . . . if I had no sense of commitment to [the South Vietnamese cause] because the Saigon government had given me no reason to have it; and if I were offered the possibility of adventure and striking at my Frenchified oppressors and their American allies, I would join up."

Shortly before this memo was written, General Westmoreland had asked for 200,000 more troops, half to come in 1967 and half in 1968. Attending to the doubts of McNamara and McPherson, Johnson gave the general only 55,000, and Johnson continued to limit the bombings to avoid antagonizing the Soviets and the Chinese. When an American plane inadvertently hit two Soviet freighters off the coast of North Vietnam, he immediately apologized to Soviet leaders and promised it wouldn't happen again.

During the summer of 1967, these dovish actions brought Johnson some relief from the antiwar protesters, whose numbers had grown steadily since 1965 as television vividly portrayed the carnage in Vietnam, including heartrending scenes of body bags returning from the field. Another factor sparing the president shouts of "Hey, hey, LBJ, how many kids did you kill today?" was the dispersal of students on summer vacation. Still another was a summit meeting Johnson held on June 21 in Glassboro, New Jersey, with the Soviet leader Aleksey Kosygin. Even though Kosygin rebuffed Johnson's peace overtures, bluntly stating that the United States should stop the bombing and get out of Vietnam, the summit demonstrated that Johnson might actually be sincere in his desire for peace.

A more serious blow to the antiwar movement in the United States had come a few weeks earlier on June 5, when Israel launched a preemptive war against Egypt, Jordan, and Syria. Israel had learned that the three countries were planning to attack, so it decided to strike first. Israel not only defeated the opposing armies but seized large hunks of land from them, occupying the Golan Heights, the West Bank, and the Sinai Peninsula, all the way to the Suez Canal.

American Jews, and the broader liberal community, most of whom still identified with Israel, found themselves admiring and even proud of Israel's success. This pride made it difficult for them to quickly shift back into a posture of antiwar righteousness on Vietnam. It was equally hard to ridicule Johnson's claim of a worldwide Communist threat when the Soviet Union had clearly been up to mischief with the Syrians and the Egyptians, whose armies they had largely equipped. All this took a bit of the heat off Lyndon Johnson.

But the antiwar movement regained momentum in the fall of

1967 as students returned to their campuses, where once again they could gather to demonstrate for peace. The students were joined by an increasing number, if still not a majority, of their parents. And perhaps most important of all, the peace movement was able to recruit a presidential candidate to oppose Johnson in the 1968 Democratic primaries: Eugene McCarthy, a U.S. senator from Minnesota and an intellectual who had won public attention with his eloquent speech on behalf of Adlai Stevenson at the 1960 Democratic Convention.

McCarthy's reputation as a thinker, combined with his stand against the war, won him the support of much of the academic elite and of the New York intellectuals who wrote for the *New York Review of Books*, a publication that had after its birth in 1963 quickly become their bible. (The *Partisan Review*, their previous home, had in their view become too rigidly anti-Communist.) McCarthy also attracted the support of thousands of idealistic students who opposed the war.

Prominent among those who joined McCarthy's campaign was Richard Goodwin, the former adviser to John Kennedy and Lyndon Johnson and the author of some of Johnson's best speeches. He had left the White House primarily because of his growing doubts about the war but also because of his distaste for Johnson as a person. Goodwin had been the first of a parade of aides who left the Johnson administration. In 1966, three of the most influential members of the staff, McGeorge Bundy, Jack Valenti, and Bill Moyers, departed.

Johnson had never been an easy man to work for. And the stress of Vietnam, like the stress of the 1960 campaign, made him even more abusive and demanding. He described his ideal staffer as "someone who will kiss my ass in Macy's window and stand up and say, 'Boy, wasn't that sweet.'" No one met this standard more precisely than Jack Valenti, who went on to become a legendarily effective lobbyist for the movie industry. His obituary in the *Washington Post* explains: "Valenti was often described as Johnson's chief whipping post, or 'glorified valet' who loyally absorbed Johnson's foul-mouthed tantrums and such seemingly humiliating acts as Johnson using Valenti's lap as a footrest."

The future Speaker of the House Thomas P. "Tip" O'Neill told of the time Valenti arrived late at a meeting Johnson was holding with the Massachusetts congressional delegation.

"Where the hell were you?" demanded Johnson.

"I was getting a cup of coffee," Valenti replied.

"You asshole," exploded Johnson, "I told you never to leave my office."

The president then proceeded to further "chastise and humiliate Valenti," in O'Neill's words, before the entire delegation.

Still, Valenti found himself able to say "How sweet it was," even going so far as to declare, in a 1965 speech, "I sleep each night a little better, a little more confidently, because Lyndon Johnson is my president." But his sleep might really have been sounder if Johnson had stopped phoning him at all hours of the night.

Johnson's behavior could be disgusting. He would, for example, require staff members to accompany him to the bathroom, where he would proceed to defecate in their presence. He also demanded that his subordinates join him for nude swimming in the White House pool. Johnson was enormously proud of his large penis (which he called Jumbo) and delighted in humiliating his less-well-endowed associates by requiring them to reveal their relative inadequacy.

Why would his subordinates put up with such behavior? One explanation is that Johnson could also be kind and generous. Joseph Califano tells of the time when Johnson discovered that his first-generation Italian-American parents were visiting Washington. Johnson invited them to a black-tie state dinner at the White House honoring the president of Italy. When he discovered that Califano's mother didn't have a suitable dress, the former aide recalled, Johnson "arranged for a White House car to take her to Garfinckel's, a fashionable Washington department store, where he insisted on purchasing an evening gown and all the trimmings at his expense."

For most of his subordinates, feelings about their leader were ambivalent. Bill Moyers would later say, "I both loved and loathed him." George Reedy said that Johnson could be "magnificent and inspiring" but also "a bully, sadist, lout, and egoist." Califano recalled him as "caring and crude, generous and petulant, bluntly honest, and calculatingly devious." Even the superloyal Valenti could couple praise of Johnson with the acknowledgment that "he was also one tough son of a bitch and he was a hard, cruel man at times."

Some of those who left even doubted Johnson's sanity. Goodwin was one, Moyers another. In December 1967, while serving as the publisher of *Newsday* in Garden City, Long Island, Moyers was having lunch with a friend. The friend, worried about Johnson's failure to face facts in Vietnam, asked Moyers, "What's wrong with him?" Moyers leaned over and whispered, "He's crazy."

Moyers's doubts about the war had led to a steady decline in his influence over Johnson before he finally announced his resignation in December 1966. Similarly, Robert McNamara's doubts had grown during 1966 and 1967, leading to Johnson's decision to replace him with Clark Clifford and arrange for McNamara to be made the president of the World Bank.

As 1967 came to a close, most of the doves had departed the administration, and the hawks seemed in control. Encouraged by American victories in battles against the Viet Cong and North Vietnamese during the fall of 1967, General Westmoreland declared, "We have got our opponent almost on the ropes. We are confident that we are winning this war."

Just before Christmas 1967, Johnson left for a trip around the world that displayed his ambivalence about the war. First, in visits to American bases in Thailand and Vietnam, he assured American troops that he would not "shimmy" in his pursuit of victory. From there, he flew to Rome, where he sought the pope's help in achieving peace. Johnson's message to the troops, observed Hugh Sidey in *Life* magazine, "seemed diluted at the Vatican where he implied that he was ready for reasonable compromise." Johnson completed his 26,959-mile trip in eighty-three hours but, in Sidey's words, "left no clear message except that Johnson was in seven league boots, striding across the Earth breaking all records."

Even as Johnson was circling the globe, American intelligence learned in 1967 that 40,000 North Vietnamese soldiers had moved into position to besiege the American base at Khe Sanh, just over the border in South Vietnam. General Westmoreland reinforced the base, and a major battle quickly developed. The situation reminded many observers of Dien Bien Phu, where beleaguered French forces had surrendered to the Vietnamese in 1954, ending French rule in Indochina. Johnson shared this concern. "I don't want any damn Dinbinphoo," he declared, demanding that the Joint Chiefs of Staff sign a statement of faith in General Westmoreland's ability to hold Khe Sanh.

Westmoreland got the message and poured immense resources into saving the base. American planes carrying supplies and reinforcements braved enemy fire to land on Khe Sanh's tiny airstrip. As the battle raged, the American news commentator Walter Cronkite of CBS expressed the fear that the base would fall.

That fear was groundless. Enough American firepower had been assembled at Khe Sanh that when it was combined with thunderous airstrikes on North Vietnamese positions by B-52 bombers, victory for the North became impossible.

But North Vietnam was successful in using Khe Sanh to distract Westmoreland's attention from other dangers. So when during the Tet holiday, in late January 1968, the North began its great offensive in which North Vietnamese regulars were joined by an uprising of Viet Cong throughout the country, the Americans were taken by surprise.

Bloody battles seemed to break out everywhere. In Saigon a few Viet Cong even managed to invade the American embassy compound, a scene that inspired dismay back home as Americans contrasted what they saw on television with Westmoreland's optimistic pronouncements of the previous fall. A photograph of the South Vietnamese general Nguyen Ngoc Loan firing his pistol at the head of a suspected Viet Cong whose hands were tied behind his back created a vivid impression of chaos and cruelty.

The hardest fighting happened in Hue, the ancient imperial capital of Vietnam, widely considered to be the country's most beautiful city. Televised accounts of the resulting destruction of cultural landmarks fortified the cause of antiwar activists, who argued that the United States was destroying Vietnam in order to save it.

But save it America did, at least for the time being. Courageous marines and soldiers outfought the Communists, who after two weeks of bitter struggle finally abandoned the city. Similar results were obtained throughout South Vietnam. The Americans inflicted a costly defeat on the Viet Cong, which proved to be a minor player in the rest of the war.

Nonetheless, the impression back home was devastating for Westmoreland and the Johnson administration. To Americans who had been told we were winning, pictures of soldiers hunkering down in trenches at besieged Khe Sanh, of an enemy able to penetrate the American embassy, and of the destruction in Hue seemed to contradict the administration's optimism. Walter Cronkite was so shocked that he asked, "What the hell is going on? I thought we were winning the war."

Peter Braestrup, one of the reporters who covered Vietnam for the *New York Times*, later wrote a book, *Big Story*, in which he assembled impressive evidence to support his thesis that the American press had turned the reality of a Tet victory for America into the illusion of a catastrophic defeat. Whatever the merits of his argument, the Tet Offensive had an impact like no other event in the war. A mood of gloom descended on Washington, a feeling that the United States was locked into a war that was hopeless—not only hopeless but wrong, with a president who was either unwilling or unable to extricate himself and the country.

As February 1968 came to a close, the same conclusion was being reached by many others throughout the country. Then came the New Hampshire primary in March, and the gloom was lifted by the seemingly miraculous showing of Eugene McCarthy, the senator the antiwar movement had persuaded to oppose Lyndon Johnson.

Here again the way the press reported the event proved crucial. Johnson's name was not on the ballot. He was a write-in candidate, and write-ins rarely obtain 10 percent of the total vote, much less win. Still, in New Hampshire, Johnson's write-in candidacy prevailed by a margin of 49 to 42 percent. But just as they had turned a Tet victory into defeat, the press transformed a Johnson victory into a Johnson loss.

The impression of Johnson's defeat, erroneous or not, galvanized the peace movement. Later in March, Robert Kennedy decided to enter the presidential race. Johnson's "wise men," an informal but influential group of friends and former high government officials, met in Washington. This group had been hawkish as recently as four months earlier but now told Johnson that the war could not be won and that peace negotiations were imperative. Even Johnson's daughter Lynda, whose husband, Chuck Robb, a marine lieutenant, had just left for Vietnam, now asked her father, "Why do we have to fight over there when so many people are opposed to the war?" Larry O'Brien, a political adviser to the president, warned him that he would be defeated in the Wisconsin primary scheduled for early April. By the end of March only 36 percent of the people approved of Johnson's presidency and only 26 percent approved of his handling of Vietnam. Faced with these numbers, Lyndon Johnson decided to take a dramatic step to demonstrate his selfless desire for peace and incidentally to spare himself the humiliation of defeat in the primaries.

Just after midnight on Sunday, March 31, a White House operator called a former Johnson aide, Horace Busby, and asked him to report to the Oval Office at nine o'clock that morning. Unlike the rest of the nation, Busby had a good idea of what to expect. Johnson, while keeping his intention from others, had asked Busby to draft an announcement of his withdrawal from the race.

When Busby arrived at the White House, Johnson told him he planned to make the announcement in a speech that evening. At 10:00 a.m. Johnson went to Hubert Humphrey's apartment and gave him the news. He then checked to see if John Connally, who had already advised him to withdraw, had changed his mind. Connally had not. That night, he addressed the nation, announcing his decision to stop the bombing of North Vietnam. "I have concluded that I should not permit the presidency to become involved in the partisan divisions that are developing in this political year," he said. "With America's sons in the fields far away, with America's future under challenge right here at home, with our hopes and the world's hopes for peace in the balance every day, I do not believe that I should devote an hour or a day of my time to any personal partisan causes or to any duties other than the awesome duties of this office—the presidency of your country."

Then he added an unexpected passage: "Accordingly, I shall not seek, and I will not accept, the nomination of my party for another term as your president."

These words had an even more salutary effect on the country's mood than McCarthy's victory in New Hampshire. For the next few days, Johnson was cheered wherever he went. A Harris poll showed that his 36 percent approval rating of the prior week had risen to 56 percent. Then at 7:30 p.m. on April 4, a cruel blow was dealt to Johnson and to the nation. Martin Luther King Jr. was murdered in Memphis.

For the nation, it meant the loss of a great leader. It also brought a shattering realization that King's dream of racial reconciliation had not yet been realized. For Johnson, it meant that his four golden days of popular acclaim—he had actually been cheered when he attended a service at St. Patrick's Cathedral in New York City that Thursday morning—turned into a nightmare of race riots throughout the country, with one of the few exceptions coming in Indianapolis, where the heartfelt eloquence of Johnson's number-one rival, Robert Kennedy, succeeded in calming the local black community.

Johnson understood the disaster that had befallen him. "Everything we've gained in the last few days, we're going to lose tonight," he told his aides. Now the violence confronted him with a formidable challenge of restoring order without resorting to excessive force, which might further inflame racial tension. Johnson understood that whatever he did, the nation's mood would again be sorely troubled.

That night, he called Washington's black mayor, Walter Washington, and the black clergyman the Reverend Walter Fauntroy and sought their help in calming the capital city. He proclaimed Sunday a national day of mourning and summoned prominent black leaders to the White House for a meeting Friday morning. When they gathered in the Oval Office, he asked them to remind their people of King's message of nonviolence and challenged white Americans to "root out every trace of racism from their hearts." Later, he and the black leaders adjourned to the National Cathedral to attend a memorial service for King. By the time they emerged from the service, dark smoke hung over a large section of the city northeast of Sixteenth Street and Massachusetts Avenue. Businesses along Seventh and Fourteenth Streets were especially hard hit. Rioters seemed at first to target businesses owned by whites in predominantly black areas. But soon everything else appeared to have caught fire. The scene shocked all who saw it. General Westmoreland, who happened to be in town, observed that the city "looked worse than Saigon did during the height of the Tet Offensive."

Johnson hoped that the appearance of overwhelming force would intimidate rioters without shots being fired. Most of the 14,000 troops employed to restore order in Washington carried unloaded weapons. The tactic worked. By Sunday, the national day of mourning that Johnson had proclaimed, the violence had largely subsided. In the week that followed, Johnson managed for one last time to display his old legislative wizardry by using the grief over King's death to motivate Congress to pass the last of his civil rights bills, the Fair Housing Act.

Good news now came from an unexpected source: Vietnam. In May the long-sought negotiations between the United States and North Vietnam finally got under way in Paris. The previous month, on April 3, the North Vietnamese had announced that they were interested in having "contact" with U.S. representatives. Perhaps the North Vietnamese were motivated by the olive branch Johnson had extended in his March 31 speech and the apparent sincerity of his desire for peace, demonstrated by his withdrawal from the presidential race, or perhaps they had been dismayed by their losses from Tet. Still, it took a while for the sides to meet in person, but on May 13 negotiations between the United States and North Vietnam actually began.

The American team was led by Averell Harriman and Cyrus Vance. The fact that Johnson had selected two men known for their dovish tendencies seemed to indicate that he was now tilting away from more hawkish advisers like Walt Rostow. Further evidence came when Johnson appointed the even more dovish George Ball to replace Arthur Goldberg as the U.S. ambassador to the United Nations. Clark Clifford, however, saw Johnson as still "torn between an honorable exit and his desire not to be the first president to lose a foreign war." And when Clifford advised Johnson that the United States could not win the war and that "our hopes must go with Paris," Johnson replied that the North Vietnamese would "do no more than remain in Paris to talk rather than negotiate, until the next administration takes over."

Johnson pledged that he and his cabinet would stay out of politics during the remainder of the 1968 campaign. But he could not resist entirely. On the Democratic side, his preference for Humphrey over McCarthy or Kennedy was clear to those who knew him. As for the Republicans, he urged his friend Nelson Rockefeller to oppose Richard Nixon for the nomination.

Rockefeller did declare his candidacy, but he remained anathema to Republican conservatives. Among the Democratic candidates, Robert Kennedy created the most excitement, drawing huge, enthusiastic crowds as he campaigned in Indiana, Nebraska, Oregon, and California, where primaries were being held. McCarthy won Oregon, but Kennedy prevailed in the other races, drawing crowds so eager to touch him that an aide had to hold on to Kennedy's body to keep him from being dragged from his car.

On the night of June 4, after winning the last of the primaries in California, Robert Kennedy left the stage of the ball-
room of the Ambassador Hotel in Los Angeles, where he had
delivered his victory speech, concluding, "On to Chicago, let's
win there." As Kennedy passed through the hotel kitchen on
the way to the elevator that would take him to his room, he was
shot by Sirhan Sirhan, a Palestinian who worked there. He died
shortly after midnight on June 6, and much of the nation once
more found itself engulfed in grief.

After a service at St. Patrick's Cathedral, the funeral train
proceeded from New York to Washington, where Robert Kennedy was to be buried at Arlington National Cemetery. Television cameras along the train's route captured unforgettable
scenes of people come together to honor their hero—Boy Scouts
and veterans carrying flags and standing at attention as they
saluted the passing train, the track lined by blacks and whites,
people of all classes slowly waving their hands in mournful
respect. For Lyndon Johnson, with his intense dislike of Bobby,
the pictures must have been deeply painful, reminding him of
his own failure to unite the country.

Kennedy's assassination, coming on the heels of King's and not
even five years after his brother's, left the nation stunned and
depressed. Three heroes had been taken by assassin's bullets. For
liberals, and indeed for a good many others, 1968 became what
the journalist Jules Witcover christened it in his book: *The Year
the Dream Died*.

Since one of Johnson's reasons for not running again was his
fear that Bobby Kennedy would defeat him, Kennedy's death
opened that decision to reconsideration. July polls showed Nixon
defeating Humphrey, but at least one had Johnson beating Nixon.
And Johnson was angered by reports that some Humphrey
advisers were urging the vice president to break with Johnson on
the war. When Humphrey showed Johnson a draft of a speech

in which he would propose including the Viet Cong in peace negotiations, a position contrary to the administration's, Johnson's reaction was unambiguous. As Humphrey later recounted, Johnson said that if the vice president delivered the speech, Johnson would "destroy me for the presidency."

Right up to the convention, many of Johnson's associates believed that the president clung to the hope of being drafted by the delegates. But that summer he made a mistake that further damaged him politically.

In June, Chief Justice Earl Warren told Johnson that he planned to retire. Johnson decided to elevate to the chief justiceship his friend Abe Fortas, whom he had earlier placed on the court, and to put in the seat to be vacated by Fortas a southerner named Homer Thornberry. Johnson thought Thornberry would appease southern senators who might otherwise oppose Fortas because he was a Jew and liberal on social issues. But Fortas was also seen as a Johnson crony. Furthermore, Fortas was considered by conservatives to be soft on crime because as a lawyer in private practice he had won the decision that gave accused criminals the right to counsel in state courts.

Fortas would have been the first Jewish chief justice. (Johnson had already made history in 1967 by making Thurgood Marshall the first black justice.) But liberals, whose support for Fortas would otherwise have been assumed, were far from uniformly enthusiastic. Fortas's closeness to Johnson made them suspicious of his views on Vietnam, now a hot-button issue for those on the left, however irrelevant those views may have been to his work on the court.

Johnson won support for Fortas from such Senate eminences as Everett Dirksen and Richard Russell. But even they could not stem the tide against Fortas that gained strength from the revelation that he had accepted money from a wealthy potential litigant before the court. Many serious students of the court were also worried about the separation of powers issue, presented by the obvious fact that Fortas had continued to function as a close counselor to the president even after taking his seat on the bench in 1965. In the end, Fortas's nomination failed, dealing a serious blow to Johnson's hopes for renomination.

The coup de grâce for those hopes came in August, in the form of a riot between peace demonstrators and police at the Democratic National Convention in Chicago. Some of the demonstrators, led by Tom Hayden and Allen Ginsberg, were peaceful, but others were not. While police clearly used excessive force, they had been provoked by the more boisterous demonstrators led by Abbie Hoffman and Jerry Rubin, who called them "pigs." The demonstration exposed differences between blue-collar and college-educated Democrats that were to haunt the party for years to come. Inside the convention, the split was epitomized in a clash between Chicago's mayor Richard Daley, representing the police, and Senator Abraham Ribicoff of Connecticut, who sympathized with the demonstrators.

During a speech nominating Senator George McGovern, a last-minute candidate for the peace faction, Ribicoff looked directly at Daley, who sat only a few rows from the podium, and said: "With George McGovern we wouldn't have Gestapo tactics on the streets of Chicago."

An enraged Daley shouted back: "Fuck you, you Jew son of a bitch, you lousy motherfucker, go home."

Johnson's admirers realized that any effort to impose his renomination on the fractious convention would likely provoke another riot among the antiwar Democrats. The best the Johnson forces could do was to support Hubert Humphrey's victory over Eugene McCarthy. And even this was threatened by a last surge of support for Teddy Kennedy, but that effort faltered when Kennedy refused to run and ended with the whimper of the McGovern candidacy.

Three weeks earlier, at the Republican convention, Richard Nixon easily won over Nelson Rockefeller and a late entry by California's new governor Ronald Reagan. Nixon's image was helped immensely by the frequent spotlighting by television cameras of his pretty daughters, Tricia and Julie. Julie enhanced the picture by being accompanied by her fiancé, David Eisenhower, the attractive grandson of the much-loved former president and hero of World War II. Thus, Nixon completed his emergence from his crushing defeat in 1962 for the California governorship, not only winning the nomination but with a comfortable lead in the polls over Humphrey.

In addition to a revitalized Richard Nixon and the handicap of having to support Johnson's Vietnam policy, Humphrey faced still another obstacle—the candidacy of George Wallace. The Alabama governor had entered the presidential race as a third-party candidate in February and was now on the ballot in every state. Wallace specialized in attacking "liberals, intellectuals and longhairs" and calling for "law and order" in an appeal to whites alarmed by rioting blacks. Otherwise, Wallace's program was populist, appealing to working-class whites whose support ordinarily would go to Humphrey.

As the Chicago convention came to a close with the band playing the joyful Humphrey campaign song, "Let a Winner Lead the Way," the candidate himself looked sadly like a loser. To come back from that debacle, Humphrey needed a lot of things to go his way. He needed the endorsement of Senators Eugene McCarthy and Ted Kennedy in order to win the support of the antiwar movement. Most of all, he needed the peace negotiations in Paris to progress to the point that the American people would see the long-promised light at the end of the tunnel in the form of a peace agreement between the Americans and the North Vietnamese. Humphrey also needed to separate himself from Lyndon Johnson enough to attract the peace voters but not alienate the Johnson loyalists. He finally tried to accomplish this in a speech in Salt Lake City on September 30. But many observers thought he was dangerously late in doing so. He also incurred Johnson's rage. This meant that Johnson's support for Humphrey became lukewarm, a cooling considerably aided by Nixon's secret courting of the president.

As for the senators whose support Humphrey sought, Eugene McCarthy let Humphrey "twist in the wind" (to use a phrase that Nixon adviser John Ehrlichman would later make famous) until the middle of October. And even then his help was tepid. "I'm voting for Humphrey and think you should suffer with me," he said. Ted Kennedy did come out for Humphrey, and they made a touching TV commercial walking on the beach together at Hyannis, stirring memories of Kennedy's brothers and seeming to confer the blessing of the Kennedy family.

Unfortunately for Humphrey, the blessing had been at least temporarily devalued when earlier in October the heroine of Camelot, Jacqueline Kennedy, married Aristotle Onassis. Whatever inner merit Onassis might have possessed was betrayed in the public mind by his gangsterlike physical appearance and his reputation as a shady businessman. For many Americans, pictures of the ceremony uniting Jackie and Onassis in holy matrimony, coupled with the report that she had sold herself for $20 million, took the bloom off the rose that had been Camelot, at least for long enough to significantly reduce the impact of Teddy's help for Humphrey.

Still, by virtue of valiant campaigning, Humphrey had managed to rise in the polls to a near deadlock with Nixon as the campaign reached its final week. He had been helped in a major way by reports of progress in the Paris peace talks. Indeed, peace seemed at hand. But then Nixon's dirty tricksters went into action.

John Mitchell, who was to become Nixon's attorney general,

enlisted the aid of Anna Chennault, the widow of General Claire Chennault, the legendary commander of the Flying Tigers and the American air force in China during World War II. Anna Chennault persuaded South Vietnamese diplomats in Washington to send a message to President Nguyen Van Thieu urging him to sabotage the peace negotiations and hold out for a better deal that they promised he would get under Richard Nixon.

Johnson tried to stop the Nixon machinations by calling Senator Everett Dirksen and telling him the White House knew what Nixon was trying to do. Nixon then called Johnson and assured him, "I would never do anything to encourage Hanoi—I mean Saigon—not to come to the table." He was lying. Thieu announced he would not support the pending peace agreement, and the news appeared in the American press the weekend before the election, dashing any hopes for peace. Humphrey's momentum came to a dead stop and went into reverse. On November 2, Richard Nixon was elected president of the United States.

10

Going Home

In mid-November the Nixons came to the White House and were warmly greeted by Lyndon and Lady Bird. Nixon, who could give a Uriah Heep imitation even better than Johnson's, was obsequiously deferential to the president. At the conclusion of the meeting, Nixon announced that until Inauguration Day, January 20, Johnson would speak "not just for this administration but for the nation." Nixon added, "And for the next administration as well." Once again he lied. He continued to counsel South Vietnam not to participate in the Paris negotiations that Johnson desperately sought to restart. President Thieu finally agreed to send his people to Paris, but they delayed substantive discussion until January 20 by focusing exclusively on procedural issues.

And even though Nixon had specifically promised Johnson that he would support Johnson's efforts to ratify a nuclear proliferation treaty with the Soviet Union, he privately told Republican senators that he was against ratifying the treaty. When Johnson wanted to travel to Moscow to work on strategic arms control, the Russians were at first enthusiastic. But then they backed down. "President Johnson learned, rather bitterly," recalled

Clark Clifford, "that Nixon had secretly told the Russians he was opposed to a Johnson-Kosygin meeting."

Nonetheless, Johnson's final days in the White House had some good moments. The *Washington Post* published an editorial praising his record, and when he concluded his final address to Congress by saying, "I hope it may be said a hundred years from now that by working together, we helped to make our country more just, more just for all of the people," his former colleagues rose to give him an ovation. As he left the House chamber, the senators and congressmen sang "Auld Lang Syne."

When the Johnsons arrived back home at the ranch, the usual entourage of White House aides was not available to help them carry their luggage into the house. "The coach has turned back into a pumpkin," Lady Bird laughed.

For Johnson, laughter came less readily. He fell into a depression similar to the one he had experienced after his heart attack in 1955. Invited to the launching of the *Apollo 11* mission to the moon during the first summer of his retirement, he had every reason to expect star treatment because of his prominent role in the development of the space program. Instead, he found himself relegated to an obscure place in the bleachers, where he wilted in the sun waiting for and then listening to Vice President Spiro Agnew, the featured speaker. It must have been galling for Johnson to find himself subordinated to an obvious third-rater like Agnew, a petty crook whose corruption, revealed by federal prosecutors in 1973, after he had been reelected, would force him to resign.

Back at the ranch, Johnson gradually emerged from his depression. Lady Bird helped, inviting a parade of interesting guests to visit. And Johnson became engrossed in running the ranch and in working with the young historian Doris Kearns on his memoir about his presidency.

Managing the ranch, Johnson demanded the same effort from

his workers that he had asked of his congressional and White House aides. "We've got a chance of producing some of the finest beef in the country if we work at it," he exhorted. "But it'll mean working every minute of every day!"

As for Kearns, Johnson had met her while she served in the 1967–68 class of White House Fellows, a program that brought promising young people, usually in their late twenties or early thirties, to Washington to serve as assistants to the president and his cabinet members. While part of the program, Kearns wrote an article for the *New Republic* criticizing U.S. involvement in Vietnam. Determined to win her over, Johnson spent an increasing amount of time with Kearns, keeping her on the White House staff after her fellowship expired. Because she was a "Harvard"—one of the political scientist Richard Neustadt's graduate students—she symbolized the group that had been most critical of his presidency. She also had an unusually engaging personality.

It was clear Johnson had a crush on her, and she was fascinated by him. When he asked her to follow him to Texas to help with the memoir, she agreed. He would lie in bed in the morning, confiding in her things that he seems to have told no one else.

Little of what he said, however, made it into his book, *The Vantage Point*. He was ashamed by the quotation of some of his more colorful remarks. "What do you think this is, the tale of an uneducated cowboy?" he would say to Kearns. "It's a presidential memoir, damn it, and I've got to come out looking like a statesman, not some backwoods politician."

Perhaps motivated by something similar to his desire to communicate with this young academic, Johnson let his hair grow long. But if he sought the favor of American students, he did not win it. They still lumped him together with Richard Nixon as war criminals. To be fair to the students, it must be acknowledged that Johnson continued to support Nixon on Vietnam.

He even told one of his aides to assure Nixon's chief of staff, H. R. Haldeman, that Johnson would never reveal how Nixon had used Anna Chennault to torpedo the peace talks until Humphrey was defeated.

Johnson did not live to see American troops and prisoners of war come home in 1973. The North Vietnamese had finally been brought to serious negotiations by a tactic that had been much favored by the hawks in the Johnson administration, bombing the daylights out of Hanoi and Haiphong. But the peace provided by the Paris agreement represented no victory for the United States. The South Vietnamese proved unable to resist the North, finally collapsing in April 1975.

Johnson's heart began to act up in March 1970, when he was taken to the Brooke Army Medical Center in San Antonio with severe chest pain. In June 1972, he had a major heart attack while visiting his daughter and son-in-law Lynda and Chuck Robb, in Charlottesville, Virginia. Thereafter, he had to take nitroglycerin pills every day. When George McGovern visited him at the ranch after McGovern had won the Democratic presidential nomination that summer, he said that Johnson "struck me as a man who really knew he had something terribly wrong with him."

In December, Johnson made his last speech at the civil rights symposium at the LBJ Library in Austin. Johnson had raised the money for and supervised the building of the library, and he was immensely proud of it. On the last day of the conference, attended by civil rights leaders and Johnson loyalists, he said of his civil rights record, "I'm kind of ashamed of myself that I had six years and couldn't do more. . . . Let no one delude himself that his work is done."

He was right that more remained to be done, but he was wrong to be ashamed. He had done more for African Americans and the cause of civil rights than any president since Abraham Lincoln.

On January 22, 1973, Johnson called the switchboard at the ranch in obvious distress. Secret Service agents rushed to his side. They found him lying on the floor, not breathing. Their efforts at resuscitation failed. Lyndon Johnson was dead, at the age of sixty-four.

Johnson was buried on the banks of the Pedernales, where the grass is green and shaded with live oaks. His daughter Luci tells of an old black man who came up to her after the graveside service. When she told him how much her father loved black people, he replied: "Ma'am, you don't have to tell me he loved me, he showed he loved me."

That could serve as half of Lyndon Johnson's epitaph. The other half was also supplied by Luci when she said, "My daddy committed political suicide for that war in Vietnam."

Why did he do it?

The answer lies in a fear he confided to Doris Kearns. If he had abandoned South Vietnam, he said, "There would be Robert Kennedy out in front, leading the fight against me, telling everyone that I had betrayed John Kennedy's commitment to South Vietnam. That I had let democracy fall into the hands of the Communists. That I was a coward, an unmanly man, a man without a spine. Oh, I could see it coming all right. Every night when I fell asleep, I could see myself tied to the ground in the middle of a long open space. In the distance I could hear the voices of thousands of people. They were all shouting at me and running towards me: 'Coward! Traitor! Weakling!'"

The genuine grief at Johnson's graveside did not represent the feelings of most of the American people. They did not love him. Most thought he was a crude politician in whom they saw none of the wit and grace of John Kennedy or the passion for social justice shared by Robert Kennedy and Martin Luther King Jr.—all leaders whose passing had been widely mourned. These men had inspired the nation with their speeches. When

Johnson spoke in public, his language was stilted and formal and his delivery dull.

History has gradually taken a kinder view. The title of the last volume of Robert Dallek's biography of Johnson, *Flawed Giant*, expresses the verdict increasingly adopted by scholars. It seems likely that history will rank Johnson in the group of presidents just below the top tier of George Washington, Abraham Lincoln, and Franklin Roosevelt. Of those in the next tier, which certainly includes Thomas Jefferson, Andrew Jackson, and Theodore Roosevelt, Johnson most resembles Jackson, another crude frontiersman whose noble stand against Nullification was marred by his terrible treatment of the Cherokee Nation.

Of all our presidents, only Franklin Roosevelt can match Johnson's legislative record. Consider just two of the many laws Johnson got passed: Medicare, which saved older Americans from a cruel choice between untreated illness and medical bills they could not afford; and the Voting Rights Act of 1965, which finally gave African Americans real political power, power that they have been able to exercise to help make one of their own president of the United States.

The skill and tenacity Johnson demonstrated in pushing his Great Society program through Congress remain unmatched. His tactics included guile—for example, he once cautioned a senator not to reveal their conversation to another senator because the latter's considerable ego might be threatened—and persistence. When House leaders called to inform him that the Ways and Means Committee had favorably reported his Medicare bill, Johnson made triple sure they knew how strongly he felt about moving the bill to the floor quickly so that it could be passed by the full House. In succession, he warned the committee's chairman, Wilbur Mills; Majority Leader Carl Albert; and finally Speaker John McCormack of the danger of delay: "For God's sake! 'Don't let dead cats stand on your porch,'

Mr. Rayburn used to say. They stunk and they stunk and they stunk." Johnson reminded them that delay would give opponents an opportunity to regroup and renew their attack.

The credit Johnson is now given for his towering record on domestic matters is usually accompanied by the blame he receives for Vietnam. And Vietnam cannot be dismissed as a minor mistake. When a Johnson admirer remarked to John Kenneth Galbraith that Johnson would have been a great president except for Vietnam, Galbraith said, "That's like saying Switzerland would be a flat country except for the Alps."

The question is: To what extent does Johnson deserve the blame for Vietnam? During all but the final year of his presidency, his Vietnam policy enjoyed the support of a majority of Democrats and Republicans in Congress and most of the people as reflected in public opinion polls. In other words, the country as a whole was complicit in the decisions that led to the tragedy—as were not just the majority but all but one (George Ball) of the national security advisers Johnson had inherited from John Kennedy. Even the antiwar movement, which was quick to protest Johnson's bombing of North Vietnam, failed to protest the escalation of the ground war in 1965, an escalation that led to the deaths of most of the Americans and Vietnamese killed by the war.

The truth is that Johnson made repeated attempts to obtain peace in Vietnam. He never tried to invade North Vietnam as Harry Truman—to whom history has been so kind in recent years—had made the mistake of invading North Korea. But even though he respected the North's territorial integrity, the North did not respect the South's. It insisted that all of Vietnam be united under Communist rule, something that many South Vietnamese did not want, as they proved by fleeing in dangerously rickety boats after the Communists took over in 1975. But the South's population also included many neutralists and members of the Viet Cong, meaning that the North was more united in the pursuit of total victory. Furthermore, the government of South Vietnam, though often changed, stayed corrupt and inefficient and unable to command the loyalty of its people. This meant that ultimately the South was going to lose and that all Johnson would accomplish by continuing the war was the death of more Americans and Vietnamese. Johnson's failure comes down to the simple fact that he could not bear to lose a war. He was wrong. Still what he did was understandable for a man reared on the legend of the Alamo, who had heard Winston Churchill tell Adolf Hitler, "We shall never surrender." Add to these apparent lessons of history Johnson's obsessive fear of being seen as a coward and his misunderstanding of the Kennedys—partly their fault, partly his—and one had all the ingredients necessary to produce tragedy.

Another nagging fact about Johnson remains: his abusive behavior toward his subordinates. The repeated public humiliation he heaped on those who loyally served him is hard to forgive. When asked to explain it, one former mistress who remained loyal to him attributes the ugly behavior to his insecurities. She does not elaborate, but it does seem possible that in moments of stress Johnson would project his own self-doubt into doubt about those around him. Another friend, Liz Carpenter, Lady Bird's press secretary, who was affectionately regarded in Washington for her humor and common sense, says: "That's just him. You have to face the fact that he was that way. You had to accept him warts and all." And so does history.

Notes

1: EARLY LIFE

2   "My ancestors were teachers and lawyers": Robert Dallek, *Lone Star Rising: Lyndon Johnson and His Times, 1908–1960* (New York: Oxford University Press, 1991), p. 14.

2   "one of the first things": Doris Kearns Goodwin, *Lyndon Johnson and the American Dream* (New York: St. Martin's Press, 1976), pp. 22–23.

3   "For days after I quit those lessons": Ibid., p. 25.

3   "the Johnson freeze-out": Ibid.

3   "sweet" and "gentle": George Reedy, *Lyndon B. Johnson: A Memoir* (New York: Andrews & McMeel, 1982), p. 34.

3   "would include such adjectives": Ibid., p. 33.

4   "We drove in the Model T Ford": Goodwin, *Lyndon Johnson and the American Dream*, pp. 36–37.

5   "I was tremendously fond of him": Randall B. Woods, *LBJ: Architect of American Ambition* (New York: Free Press, 2006), p. 57.

5   "A cross between": Ibid., p. 55.

6   "marathon talk about political personalities": Dallek, *Lone Star Rising*, p. 71.

6   "with long, loping strides": Goodwin, *Lyndon Johnson and the American Dream*, p. 47.

6   "like the seat of his britches": Dallek, *Lone Star Rising*, p. 67.

6   "he could look busy doing nothing": Ibid.

6   "was going somewhere": Robert Dallek, *Lyndon B. Johnson: Portrait of a President* (New York: Penguin Books, 2004), p. 12.

6   "he'd just interrupt you": Robert A. Caro, *The Path to Power: The Years of Lyndon Johnson* (New York: Alfred A. Knopf, 1982), p. 154.

7   "shiftless dirt farmers": Ronnie Dugger, *The Politician: The Life and Times of Lyndon Johnson* (New York: W. W. Norton, 1982), p. 124.

7   "just worse than you'd treat a dog": Dallek, *Lyndon B. Johnson*, p. 16.

7   "going through a garbage pile": Woods, *LBJ*, p. 63.

8   "I took my first paycheck": Dugger, *The Politician*, p. 116.

8   "His being there": Woods, *LBJ*, p. 64.

8   "the kind of teacher": Ibid.

8   "tremendously": Dallek, *Lone Star Rising*, p. 80.

8   "You never forgot what poverty": Woods, *LBJ*, p. 63.

8   "one of the very best": Ibid., p. 65.

9   "I wanted to finish": Ibid.

9   "I rode all the byways": Ibid., p. 69.

9   "as if his life depended on it": Dallek, *Lone Star Rising*, p. 89.

10   "He turned to me and said": Woods, *LBJ*, p. 74.

10   "If I were a young man": Ibid., p. 73.

2: MR. JOHNSON COMES TO WASHINGTON

12   "Maybe Sam Johnson's boy": Merle Miller, *Lyndon: An Oral Biography* (New York: Ballantine Books, 1980), p. 51.

12   "People know when you're sick": Goodwin, *Lyndon Johnson and the American Dream*, p. 89. Whenever he was at the ranch, Johnson "loved to roam the countryside, stopping off here and there at neighbors in order to visit Cousin Oriole or Mr. Hodges. . . . [He] kept up with the family news on all his neighbors—births, deaths and ailments—and fulfilled his father's description exactly" (Liz Carpenter, *Ruffles and Flourishes* [New York: Doubleday, 1969], p. 171).

13   "White was a Texan too": Russell Baker, e-mail to author, September 1, 2007.

14   "the Communists hoped to incite": Stephen E. Ambrose, *Eisenhower: Soldier, General of the Army, President-Elect, 1890–1952* (New York: Simon and Schuster, 1983), p. 97.

14   "were quiet and orderly": Ibid.

14   "I just can't understand how such a damn fool": Ibid.

14   "like sheep by a man": Dallek, *Lone Star Rising*, p. 105.

15   "I felt a little": Goodwin, *Lyndon Johnson and the American Dream*, p. 80.

16   "Daughter, you've been bringing home": Ibid., p. 82.
16   "Let's get married": Ibid.
18   "Johnson was operating the best": Dallek, *Lone Star Rising*, p. 143.
18   "Of course there will be those": Ibid., p. 147.
19   "When I come back to Washington": Dugger, *The Politician*, p. 185.
19   "came on like a freight train": Dallek, *Lone Star Rising*, p. 160.
19   "I've just met the most remarkable": Ibid., p. 161.
20   "He got more projects": Dallek, *Lyndon B. Johnson*, p. 39.
21   "the most beautiful woman": Caro, *Path to Power*, p. 480.
22   "her long blond hair floating": Jennet Conant, *The Irregulars: Roald Dahl and the British Spy Ring in Wartime Washington* (New York: Simon and Schuster, 2008), p. 159.
23   "They didn't let her": Ibid., p. 169.

3: TRYING FOR THE SENATE

25   "I can't take part": Woods, *LBJ*, p. 146.
27   "As a member of the Naval Reserve": Ibid., p. 162.
27   "It is time to quit 'conferring' and go to work": Ibid.
28   "cool as a cucumber": Ibid., p. 167.
28   "just as calm as if we were on a sightseeing tour": Robert A. Caro, *Means of Ascent: The Years of Lyndon Johnson* (New York: Alfred A. Knopf, 1990), p. 43.
28   "an absolute physical coward": Caro, *Path to Power*, p. 156.
30   "Please make it before election day": David M. Kennedy, *Freedom from Fear: The American People in Depression and War, 1929–1945* (New York: Oxford University Press, 2005), p. 579.
31   "Who's that": Woods, *LBJ*, p. 171.
31   "Tess" and "Miss Jesus": Ibid., p. 168.
31   "I want that house": Caro, *Means of Ascent*, p. 70.
31   "I'd buy the house": Ibid., p. 71.
32   "not for the needy": Dallek, *Lone Star Rising*, p. 258.
33   "irresponsible, racketeering, self-inflated labor leaders": Ibid., p. 288.
35   "cold, cold as a February iceberg": Ruth McCormick Simms, quoted in Charles Peters, *Five Days in Philadelphia* (New York: PublicAffairs, 2005), p. 19.
36   "looked hopeless": Dallek, *Lone Star Rising*, p. 318.
36   "You get me off up here": Woods, *LBJ*, p. 210.

36   "evaded more issues": Miller, *Lyndon*, p. 122.
37   "the most brilliant legal mind": Caro, *Means of Ascent*, p. 11.

4: THE ART OF THE POSSIBLE

42   "Shall we have a commissioner": Robert A. Caro, *Master of the Senate: The Years of Lyndon Johnson* (New York: Alfred A. Knopf, 2002), p. 295.
45   "the biggest honeyfucking I have ever seen": Woods, *LBJ*, p. 241.
47   "Have you no sense of decency": James T. Patterson, *Grand Expectations: The United States, 1945–74* (New York: Oxford University Press, 1996), p. 269.
48   "My God, man": Dallek, *Lone Star Rising*, p. 485.
48   "I'd rather have my pecker cut off": Caro, *Master of the Senate*, p. 624.
49   "Every minute of every day": Ibid., p. 631.
50   "Lyndon loved people": Ibid., p. 654.
50   "I guess I'm used to it": Woods, *LBJ*, p. 481.
50   "The key to understanding Lady Bird": Ibid., p. 370.
53   "There comes a time": Taylor Branch, *Parting the Waters: America in the King Years, 1954–1963* (New York: Simon and Schuster, 1988), p. 805.
55   "Denial of the right": Caro, *Master of the Senate*, p. 979.
55   "Will the Senator yield?": Ibid.
55   "designed to eliminate whatever basis": Ibid.
55   "happy to accept": Ibid.
56   "I think the Senator": Ibid., p. 980.
56   "It is worse than no bill at all": Ibid., p. 991.
56   "I was so mad at Johnson I was speechless": Ibid.
56   "represents an almost universal acknowledgment": Ibid., p. 986.
57   "once Congress had lost its virginity": Ibid., p. 995.
57   "Disappointing as the Senate's version": Ibid.
57   "remained convinced that Russell": Nadine Cohodas, *Strom Thurmond and the Politics of Southern Change* (New York: Simon and Schuster, 1993), p. 299.
58   "Johnson's Masterpiece": Caro, *Master of the Senate*, p. 1005.
58   "the most remarkable feat of political generalship": Ibid., p. 1006.

5: RUNNING SECOND

60   "A Washington lawyer": Assessor's clerk to author, April 1960.
62   "answering those quorum calls": Dallek, *Lone Star Rising*, p. 574.

62 "lauded Senator Johnson's skill": Rowland Evans Jr., "The Kennedy-Johnson 'Debate,' " *New York Herald Tribune*, July 13, 1960.

62 "After Sen. Kennedy's brief effective reply": Ibid.

62 "I wasn't any Chamberlain": Woods, *LBJ*, p. 358.

63 "You Johnson people": Ibid.

63 "abrasive is an understatement": Martin F. Nolan to author, August 29, 2009.

63 "You've always hated the Kennedys": Ibid.

63 "Son, you've got to learn": Woods, *LBJ*, p. 357.

65 "Do you really want me?": Jeff Shesol, *Mutual Contempt: Lyndon Johnson, Robert Kennedy, and the Feud That Defined a Decade* (New York: W. W. Norton, 1997), p. 53.

65 "Aw, shit": Woods, *LBJ*, p. 364.

65 "Bobby's been out of touch": Shesol, *Mutual Contempt*, p. 54.

66 "side by side with Bowie and Crockett": Woods, *LBJ*, p. 369.

66 "I'm sure that they didn't ask": Ibid., p. 371.

66 "What Southern gentleman": Ibid., p. 370.

66 "What has Nixon ever done": Ibid., p. 371.

67 "LBJ Sold Out to Yankee Socialists": Ibid., p. 373.

67 "Judas": Ibid.

67 "If the time has come": Ibid.

67 "I have not seen you pay": James Rowe, "Dear Lyndon" letter, October 8, 1960. James Rowe III gave the author a copy of this letter.

68 "Now I know the difference": Miller, *Lyndon*, p. 337.

68 "I can't afford to have my vice president": Woods, *LBJ*, p. 380.

68 "Taj Majal": Ibid., p. 381.

69 "You're dealing with a very": Ibid., p. 380.

69 "our ancestors pledged": Miller, *Lyndon*, p. 353.

70 "I cannot stress too strongly": Dallek, *Lyndon B. Johnson*, p. 130.

70 "When I was a boy in Texas": Shesol, *Mutual Contempt*, p. 97.

72 "The CEEO . . . could have": Woods, *LBJ*, p. 397.

72 "We are confronted primarily": "Transcript of the President's Address," *New York Times*, June 12, 1963.

72 "He's damn good": Branch, *Parting the Waters*, p. 883.

72 "manned exploration of the moon": Woods, *LBJ*, p. 393.

74 "There are some people who like to look crooked": Ibid., pp. 412–13.

74 "hardly knew Bobby Baker": Ibid., p. 526.

75 "My brother and I extend": Shesol, *Mutual Contempt*, p. 148.

76 "You can't say that Dallas": Woods, *LBJ*, p. 417.

78   "People don't realize how conservative": Shesol, *Mutual Contempt*, p. 122.

6: A WINNING YEAR

81   "As an emotional issue": Lyndon B. Johnson, *The Vantage Point: Perspectives of the Presidency, 1963–1969* (New York: Holt, Rinehart and Winston, 1971), p. 37.

81   "a good poker player": Ibid.

81   "I knew that if I didn't get out in front": Goodwin, *Lyndon Johnson and the American Dream*, p. 191.

81   "call me whenever there's trouble": Dallek, *Lyndon B. Johnson*, p. 165.

82   "You will recognize the words": Ibid., p. 164.

82   "the South to the Republican Party": Woods, *LBJ*, p. 480.

83   "I would have kissed [his] ass": Ibid., p. 474.

83   "Stronger than all the armies": Ibid., p. 478.

87   "Vietnam will collapse": Ibid., p. 508.

87   "We can send Marines": Michael R. Beschloss, ed., *Taking Charge: The Johnson White House Tapes, 1963–1964* (New York: Simon and Schuster, 1997), p. 264.

87   "providing training and logistical support": Woods, *LBJ*, p. 508.

87   "I shudder at getting": Beschloss, *Taking Charge*, p. 363.

88   "I'd like to hear you talk": Ibid.

88   "There have been some covert operations": Ibid., p. 493.

88   "You're going to be running against a man": Ibid., p. 494.

89   "I'd tell them awfully quiet": Ibid., p. 495.

89   "personally ordered the Navy": Ibid.

89   "we have been carrying on some operations in that area": Ibid., p. 499.

90   "Vietnam was clearly an issue": Robert Dallek, *Flawed Giant: Lyndon Johnson and His Times, 1961–1973* (New York: Oxford University Press, 1998), p. 147.

91   "We're eyeball to eyeball": Patterson, *Grand Expectations*, p. 502.

91   his friends Charles Bartlett and Stewart Alsop: In 1972 the author called Bartlett to tell him about Graham Allison's revelation in the October issue of the *Washington Monthly* of John Kennedy's dovish dispatch of Robert Kennedy to tell Dobrynin that we would withdraw our missiles from Turkey. Bartlett was shocked. He could not believe what he was hearing. That Kennedy would have deceived the friend that had brought him and Jackie together suggests the extent of his desperation to conceal his dovishness and appear tough. See Graham Allison,

"Cuban Missiles and Kennedy Macho: New Evidence to Dispel the Myth," *Washington Monthly*, October 1972, pp. 14–19.

92 Robert McNamara . . . never told Johnson about it: Robert McNamara, interview with author, November 16, 2006. Theodore Sorensen provided the author with a list of those who knew about the visit. Johnson's name is not on it.

92 Perhaps the most ironic part of this story: Ernest R. May and Philip D. Zelikow, eds., *The Kennedy Tapes: Inside the White House During the Cuban Missile Crisis* (Cambridge, Mass.: Harvard University Press, 1997), p. 370.

93 "that the U.S. flinches": Beschloss, *Taking Charge*, p. 493n4.

93 "There is a limit on the number": Ibid., p. 500n6.

94 "The attacks were unprovoked": "Remarks at Syracuse University on the Communist Challenge in Southeast Asia, August 5, 1964," *Public Papers of the Presidents of the United States, Lyndon B. Johnson, 1963–64, Book II*, p. 928.

94 "like grandma's nightshirt": Dallek, *Flawed Giant*, p. 154.

94 "freak weather effects": Woods, *LBJ*, p. 515.

95 "Hell, those dumb, stupid sailors": Dallek, *Flawed Giant*, p. 155.

95 "a blank-check authorization": Beschloss, *Taking Charge*, p. 507.

95 "I've reached the conclusion": "President Bars Kennedy, Five Others from Ticket; Humphrey, M'Carthy Lead," *New York Times*, July 31, 1964.

96 "Sorry I took so many": Shesol, *Mutual Contempt*, p. 209.

96 "If you seat those": Woods, *LBJ*, p. 534.

97 "I am absolutely positive": Beschloss, *Taking Charge*, p. 529.

98 "You don't often find a man": Shesol, *Mutual Contempt*, p. 226.

98 "already one of the great presidents": Ibid.

98 "Extremism in defense of liberty is no vice": Patterson, *Grand Expectations*, p. 549.

99 "In your gut, you know he's nuts": Dallek, *Flawed Giant*, p. 170.

99 "Lady Bird Special": Woods, *LBJ*, p. 543.

99 "Robert E. Lee counseled": Ibid., p. 540.

7: THE GREAT SOCIETY

103 "corny, warm setting": Lady Bird Johnson, *A White House Diary* (New York: Holt, Rinehart and Winston, 1970), p. 259.

103 "I will never do anything": Woods, *LBJ*, p. 567.

104 "four out of five persons": Dallek, *Lyndon B. Johnson*, p. 198.

104 "invade every area of freedom": Ibid., p. 199.

105 "would be able to work something out": Ibid., p. 198.

105 "arrange for prompt hearings": Woods, *LBJ*, p. 572.

106 "Of course they'll support": Joseph A. Califano, *The Triumph and Tragedy of Lyndon Johnson* (College Station, Tex.: Texas A&M University Press, 2000), p. 50.

106 "every remaining obstacle": "Transcript of the President's Message to Congress on the State of the Union," *New York Times*, January 5, 1965.

106 "the lowest form of humanity": Dallek, *Lyndon B. Johnson*, p. 202.

107 "May we have a word": Taylor Branch, *At Canaan's Edge: America in the King Years, 1965–1968* (New York: Simon and Schuster, 2006), p. 50.

107 "littered with abandoned purses": Ibid., p. 52.

108 "Don't shit me about": Dallek, *Lyndon B. Johnson*, p. 204.

109 "enemies of justice": "Transcript of Johnson's Statement on the Arrests in Alabama," *New York Times*, March 27, 1965.

109 "There is no Negro problem": "Transcript of the Johnson Address on Voting Rights to Joint Session of Congress," *New York Times*, March 16, 1965.

110 "Manny, I want you to start hearings tonight": Branch, *At Canaan's Edge*, p. 115.

110 "cracking the whip": Miller, *Lyndon*, p. 528.

110 "strike away the last major shackle": "Text of Johnson's Statement on Voting Rights Law," *New York Times*, August 7, 1965.

110 "you keep telling people": Califano, *Triumph and Tragedy*, p. 59.

111 "Where is my immigration bill": Branch, *At Canaan's Edge*, p. 159.

8: ESCALATION

112 "Dead and dying": Woods, *LBJ*, p. 601.

112 "The event shook Bundy": Robert McNamara, interview with author, November 16, 2006.

113 "We have kept our gun over the mantel": Johnson, *Vantage Point*, p. 125.

114 "'white-faced' soldiers": Stanley Karnow, *Vietnam: A History* (New York: Penguin Books, 1983), p. 416.

114 "could [they] do much better": Ibid.

114 "I guess we've got no choice": Michael R. Beschloss, ed., *Reaching for Glory: Lyndon Johnson's Secret White House Tapes, 1964–1965* (New York: Simon and Schuster, 2001), p. 211.

114 "If they get 150": Woods, *LBJ*, p. 611.

115   "start killing the Viet Cong": Karnow, *Vietnam*, p. 418.

115   "President Plans No Major Change in Vietnam Policy": *New York Times*, April 25, 1965.

115   "plans for a major buildup of United States ground forces": Hanson Baldwin, "Build-Up Reported Planned," *New York Times*, April 21, 1965.

116   "Situation deteriorating rapidly": Woods, *LBJ*, p. 621.

116   "first military intervention": Ibid., p. 622.

116   "to sit here": Ibid.

117   "started out as a Bosch operation": Beschloss, *Reaching for Glory*, p. 297.

117   "Some 1500 innocent people": Woods, *LBJ*, p. 628.

118   "losing Cuba again": Evidence that Johnson was afraid of losing another Cuba can be found in Johnson, *Vantage Point*, p. 198 ("The last thing I wanted—and the last thing the American people wanted—was another Cuba on our doorstep," Johnson writes), and in Beschloss, *Reaching for Glory*, p. 300, where Johnson confides to Senator Mike Mansfield, "They're going to eat us up if I let another Cuba come in there."

120   "What I would like to know": Unpublished memoir by Jack Valenti given to author by Mary Margaret Valenti. Valenti attended all the meetings leading to the 1965 escalation and his account is based on the detailed notes he took during these meetings. The notes are at the Lyndon B. Johnson Library at the University of Texas, Austin. The memoir is also the source for the quotes that follow from President Johnson, Carl Rowan, Henry Cabot Lodge, Robert McNamara, McGeorge Bundy, Dean Rusk, Admiral McDonald, George Ball, and Mike Mansfield.

122   Johnson behaved with courtesy: Johnson's willingness to hear their case was one factor in keeping the dissenters from speaking out outside the government. Another was the culture of the higher levels of government, as described in James C. Thomson Jr.'s brilliant article in the April 1968 issue of the *Atlantic Monthly*. Thomson explored the interaction of that culture and the character of the men who worked in national security affairs, using concepts such as "the domestication of dissenters" and "the effectiveness trap" to explain why good men in government who were opposed to the war had not spoken out publicly. See James C. Thomson Jr., "How Could Vietnam Happen? An Autopsy," *Atlantic Monthly*, April 1968.

123   "I have today ordered": "Transcript of the President's News Conference on Foreign and Domestic Affairs," *New York Times*, July 29, 1965.

124   "Mr. Stop the Bombing": Johnson's description of Moyers was fairly common knowledge among Washington insiders in 1966, told to the author by, among others, Hayes Redmon, a top aide to Moyers at the time.

124   "I would frequently fall": Charles Peters, *How Washington Really Works*, 4th ed. (Reading, Mass.: Addison-Wesley, 1993), p. 147.

124   "I don't want to get in a war": Beschloss, *Reaching for Glory*, p. 403.

124   "President's Wife Is Near Tears": *New York Times*, July 29, 1965.

124   "this heavy load of tension": Beschloss, *Reaching for Glory*, p. 227.

124   "tormented": Dallek, *Flawed Giant*, p. 282.

125   "sleepless at night": Johnson, *Vantage Point*, p. 151.

125   "lonely vigils": Ibid.

125   "the most agonizing": "Transcript of the President's News Conference on Foreign and Domestic Affairs," *New York Times*, July 29, 1965.

127   "A divisive debate about": Johnson, *Vantage Point*, p. 152.

128   "Be sure to tell him": A former Johnson aide to the author, September 2007.

128   "not guarantee success": Robert D. Schulzinger, *A Time for War: The United States and Vietnam, 1941–1975* (New York: Oxford University Press, 1997), p. 189.

129   "appointment places beside the President": "The Rostow Appointment," *New York Times*, April 2, 1966.

129   "setbacks and losses": David Milne, *America's Rasputin: Walt Rostow and the Vietnam War* (New York: Farrar, Straus and Giroux, 2008), p. 167.

130   "may become the first in a series of steps": Shesol, *Mutual Contempt*, p. 286.

130   "arrogance of power": Karnow, *Vietnam*, p. 486.

130   "Not a Dove, but No Longer a Hawk": Neil Sheehan, *New York Times Magazine*, October 9, 1966.

9: A CULTURAL REVOLUTION

135   "basically a subsistence agricultural economy": Karnow, *Vietnam*, pp. 499–500.

135   "no reasonable way to bring": Woods, *LBJ*, p. 735.

135   "nail the coonskin to the wall": Rick Pearlstein, *Nixonland: The Rise of a President and the Fracturing of America* (New York: Scribner, 2008), p. 155.

135   "stand firm": "Text of Message by President Johnson to Con-

gress on the State of the Union," *New York Times*, January 11, 1967, provided to the author by McPherson.

136 "bomb, bomb, bomb": Karnow, *Vietnam*, p. 504.

136 "Senator Halfbright": Ibid., p. 503.

136 "It sounds romantic to say so": Harry McPherson, Memorandum for the President, June 13, 1967, provided to the author by McPherson.

138 "someone who will kiss my ass": Caro, *Master of the Senate*, p. 129.

139 "Valenti was often described": Adam Bernstein, "A Hollywood Promoter on Both Coasts," *Washington Post*, April 27, 2007.

139 "Where the hell were you": Tip O'Neill with William Novak, *Man of the House: The Life and Political Memoirs of Speaker Tip O'Neill* (New York: Random House, 1987), p. 184.

139 "I sleep each night a little better": Bernstein, "Hollywood Promoter on Both Coasts."

139 which he called Jumbo: Caro, *Master of the Senate*, p. 121.

140 "arranged for a White House car": Califano, *Triumph and Tragedy*, p. 336.

140 "I both loved and loathed him": Bill Moyers, quoted by Harry McPherson to author, November 18, 2008.

140 "a bully, sadist": Reedy, *Lyndon B. Johnson*, p. 157.

140 "caring and crude": Joseph A. Califano Jr., *Inside: A Public and Private Life* (New York: PublicAffairs, 2004), p. 159.

140 "he was also one tough son of a bitch": Woods, *LBJ*, p. 645.

140 "He's crazy": Bill Moyers, conversation with author, December 1967.

140 "We have got our opponent": Dallek, *Lyndon B. Johnson*, p. 315.

141 "shimmy": Hugh Sidey, "Around the World with Lyndon B. Magellan," *Life*, January 5, 1968.

141 "seemed diluted at the Vatican": Ibid.

141 "left no clear message": Ibid.

141 "I don't want any damn Dinbinphoo": Karnow, *Vietnam*, p. 541.

143 "What the hell is going on": Woods, *LBJ*, p. 825.

144 "Why do we have to fight over there": Branch, *At Canaan's Edge*, p. 747.

144 "I have concluded that I should not permit the presidency": Lyndon B. Johnson, Address to the Nation, March 31, 1968, accessible at http://www.lbjlib.utexas.edu/Johnson/archives .hom/speeches.hom/680331.asp.

145 "Everything we've gained": Dallek, *Lyndon B. Johnson*, p. 334.

146 "root out every trace of racism": Woods, *LBJ*, p. 839.

146   "looked worse than Saigon": Ibid.
147   "torn between an honorable exit": Dallek, *Lyndon B. Johnson*,
       p. 335.
147   "our hopes must go with Paris": Ibid., p. 337.
147   "do no more than remain in Paris": Ibid.
148   "On to Chicago": "Kennedy Shot and Gravely Wounded After
       Winning California Primary; Suspect Seized in Los Angeles
       Hotel," *New York Times*, June 5, 1968.
149   "destroy me for the presidency": Dallek, *Flawed Giant*, p. 571.
150   "With George McGovern": Patterson, *Grand Expectations*,
       p. 696.
150   "Fuck you, you Jew son of a bitch": Ibid.
151   "liberals, intellectuals and longhairs": Ibid., p. 699.
151   "law and order": Ibid., p. 698.
152   "I'm voting for Humphrey": Woods, *LBJ*, p. 874.
153   "I would never do anything": Ibid., p. 875.

                           10: GOING HOME

154   "not just for this administration": Woods, *LBJ*, pp. 876–77.
154   "President Johnson learned, rather bitterly": Dallek, *Lyndon B.
       Johnson*, p. 360.
155   "I hope it may be said": "Transcript of President's State of the
       Union Message to Joint Session of Congress," *New York Times*,
       January 15, 1969.
155   "The coach has turned": Johnson, *Vantage Point*, p. 568.
156   "We've got a chance of producing": Goodwin, *Lyndon Johnson
       and the American Dream*, p. 360.
156   "What do you think this is": Ibid., p. 355.
157   "struck me as a man": Woods, *LBJ*, p. 883.
157   "I'm kind of ashamed": Ibid., pp. 883–84.
158   "Ma'am, you don't have to tell": Ibid., p. 884.
158   "My daddy committed political suicide": Dallek, *Lyndon B.
       Johnson*, p. 362.
158   "There would be Robert Kennedy out in front": Goodwin, *Lyn-
       don Johnson and the American Dream*, p. 253.
159   "For God's sake!": Beschloss, *Reaching for Glory*, p. 242.
160   "That's like saying": Stephen Schlossberg, former general
       counsel of the United Auto Workers, to author, September 2009.
161   "That's just him": Liz Carpenter to author, telephone conversa-
       tion, September 2009.

Milestones

1908   Lyndon Baines Johnson is born on August 27 to Rebekah Baines Johnson and Sam Ealy Johnson at their home between Hye and Stonewall, Texas

1924   Completes high school in Johnson City

1927   Enters Southwest Texas State Teachers College at San Marcos

1929   Teaches school in Cotulla, Texas

1930   Graduates from college, teaches at Sam Houston High School in Houston

1931   Joins staff of Representative Richard Kleberg in Washington

1934   Marries Claudia Alta (Lady Bird) Taylor

1935   Appointed Texas state director for the National Youth Administration

1937   Elected to the U.S. House of Representatives

1941   Fails in run for U.S. Senate

1942   Serves in U.S. Navy for six months, returns to House of Representatives

1944   Daughter Lynda born

1947   Daughter Luci born

1948   Elected to the U.S. Senate

1951	Becomes majority whip in the U.S. Senate
1953	Becomes minority leader in the U.S. Senate
1955	Becomes majority leader in the U.S. Senate; censure of Senator Joseph McCarthy; suffers heart attack
1957	Passage of the Civil Rights Act of 1957
1960	Elected vice president of the United States
1963	Becomes president of the United States upon the assassination of John F. Kennedy in Dallas on November 22
1964	Passage of the Civil Rights Act of 1964, the Economic Opportunity Act of 1964, and Tonkin Gulf Resolution; wins full term as president by defeating Senator Barry Goldwater
1965	Passage of Medicare, the Immigration Act of 1965, and the Voting Rights Act of 1965; first ground troops are sent to Vietnam, major escalation of war in July
1968	Announces he will not run for reelection; assassinations of Martin Luther King Jr. and Robert Kennedy; Richard Nixon elected successor
1969	Leaves Washington, retires to ranch on Pedernales
1973	Dies at ranch on January 22

Selected Bibliography

Ambrose, Stephen E. *Eisenhower: Soldier, General of the Army, President-Elect, 1890–1952.* New York: Simon and Schuster, 1983.

Baker, Bobby, with Larry L. King. *Wheeling and Dealing: Confessions of a Capitol Hill Operator.* New York: W. W. Norton, 1978.

Barnes, Ben, with Lisa Dickey. *Barn Burning, Barn Building: Tales of a Political Life, From LBJ to George Bush and Beyond.* Albany, Tex.: Bright Sky Press, 2006.

Beschloss, Michael R., ed. *Reaching for Glory: Lyndon Johnson's Secret White House Tapes, 1964–1965.* New York: Simon and Schuster, 2001.

———. *Taking Charge: The Johnson White House Tapes, 1963–1964.* New York: Simon and Schuster, 1997.

Braestrup, Peter. *Big Story: How the American Press and Television Reported and Interpreted the Crisis of Tet 1968 in Vietnam and Washington,* vols. 1 and 2. Boulder, Colo.: Westview Press, 1977.

Branch, Taylor. *At Canaan's Edge: America in the King Years, 1965–1968.* New York: Simon and Schuster, 2006.

———. *Parting the Waters: America in the King Years, 1954–1963.* New York: Simon and Schuster, 1988.

Brinkley, Alan. *Voices of Protest: Huey Long, Father Coughlin, and the Great Depression.* New York: Alfred A. Knopf, 1982.

Brokaw, Tom. *Boom!: Voices of the Sixties.* New York: Random House, 2007.

Busby, Horace. *The Thirty-first of March: An Intimate Portrait of Lyndon Johnson's Final Days in Office.* New York: Farrar, Straus and Giroux, 2005.

Califano, Joseph A., Jr. *Inside: A Public and Private Life*. New York: PublicAffairs, 2004.

———. *The Triumph and Tragedy of Lyndon Johnson*. College Station, Tex.: Texas A&M University Press, 2000.

Caro, Robert A. *Master of the Senate: The Years of Lyndon Johnson*. New York: Alfred A. Knopf, 2002.

———. *Means of Ascent: The Years of Lyndon Johnson*. New York: Alfred A. Knopf, 1990.

———. *The Path to Power: The Years of Lyndon Johnson*. New York: Alfred A. Knopf, 1982.

Carpenter, Liz. *Ruffles and Flourishes*. Garden City, N.Y.: Doubleday, 1970.

Cohodas, Nadine. *Strom Thurmond and the Politics of Southern Change*. New York: Simon and Schuster, 1993.

Conant, Jennet. *The Irregulars: Roald Dahl and the British Spy Ring in Wartime Washington*. New York: Simon and Schuster, 2008.

Conkin, Paul K. *Big Daddy from the Pedernales: Lyndon Baines Johnson*. Boston: Twayne, 1986.

Connally, John, with Mickey Herskowitz. *In History's Shadow: An American Odyssey*. New York: Hyperion, 1993.

Dallek, Robert. *Flawed Giant: Lyndon Johnson and His Times, 1961–1973*. New York: Oxford University Press, 1998.

———. *Lone Star Rising: Lyndon Johnson and His Times, 1908–1960*. New York: Oxford University Press, 1991.

———. *Lyndon B. Johnson: Portrait of a President*. New York: Penguin Books, 2004.

Danbom, David B. *Born in the Country*. Baltimore: Johns Hopkins University Press, 1995.

Dobbs, Michael. *One Minute to Midnight: Kennedy, Khrushchev, and Castro on the Brink of Nuclear War*. New York: Vintage Books, 2009.

Dugger, Ronnie. *The Politician: The Life and Times of Lyndon Johnson*. New York: W. W. Norton, 1982.

Gillon, Steven M. *The Kennedy Assassination—24 Hours After: Lyndon B. Johnson's Pivotal First Day as President*. New York: Basic Books, 2009.

Goldstein, Gordon M. *Lessons in Disaster: McGeorge Bundy and the Path to War in Vietnam*. New York: Times Books, 2008.

Goodwin, Doris Kearns. *Lyndon Johnson and the American Dream*. New York: St. Martin's Press, 1976.

Goodwin, Richard N. *Remembering America: A Voice from the Sixties*. Boston: Little, Brown, 1988.

Guthman, Edwin O., and Jeffrey Shulman, eds. *Robert Kennedy in His Own Words: The Unpublished Recollections of the Kennedy Years*. New York: Bantam Books, 1988.

Hahn, Steven, and Jonathan Prude, eds. *The Countryside in the Age of Capitalist Transformation*. Chapel Hill, N.C.: University of North Carolina Press, 1985.

Halberstam, David. *The Best and the Brightest*. London: Barrie and Jenkins, 1972.

Humphrey, Hubert H. *The Education of a Public Man: My Life and Politics*. Edited by Norman Sherman. Garden City, N.Y.: Doubleday, 1976.

Isaacson, Walter, and Evan Thomas. *The Wise Men: Six Friends and the World They Made*. New York: Simon and Schuster, 1986.

Johnson, Lady Bird. *A White House Diary*. New York: Holt, Rinehart and Winston, 1970.

Johnson, Lyndon Baines. *The Vantage Point: Perspectives of the Presidency, 1963–1969*. New York: Holt, Rinehart and Winston, 1971.

Johnson, Paul. *Modern Times: The World from the Twenties to the Eighties*. New York: Harper and Row, 1983.

Jones, Howard. *Death of a Generation: How the Assassinations of Diem and JFK Prolonged the Vietnam War*. New York: Oxford University Press, 2003.

Karnow, Stanley. *Vietnam: A History*. New York: Penguin Books, 1983.

Kennedy, David M. *Freedom from Fear: The American People in Depression and War, 1929–1945*. New York: Oxford University Press, 2005.

Kennedy, Robert F. *Thirteen Days: A Memoir of the Cuban Missile Crisis*. New York: W. W. Norton, 1969.

Kotz, Nick. *Judgment Days: Lyndon Baines Johnson, Martin Luther King Jr. and the Laws That Changed America*. Boston: Houghton Mifflin, 2005.

Lemann, Nicholas. *The Promised Land: The Great Black Migration and How It Changed America*. New York: Alfred A. Knopf, 1991.

Mackenzie, G. Calvin, and Robert Weisbrot. *The Liberal Hour: Washington and the Politics of Change in the 1960s*. New York: Penguin Press, 2008.

Manchester, William. *The Death of a President*. New York: Harper and Row, 1967.

———. *The Glory and the Dream: A Narrative History of America, 1932–1972*. Boston: Little, Brown, 1973.

May, Ernest R., and Philip D. Zelikow, eds. *The Kennedy Tapes: Inside the White House During the Cuban Missile Crisis*. Cambridge, Mass.: Harvard University Press, 1997.

McCullough, David. *Truman*. New York: Simon and Schuster, 1992.

McMaster, H. R. *Dereliction of Duty*. New York: HarperCollins, 1997.

McNamara, Robert S., with Brian VanDeMark. *In Retrospect: The Tragedy and Lessons of Vietnam*. New York: Vintage Books, 1996.

McPherson, Harry C. *A Political Education*. Boston: Little, Brown, 1972.

Miller, Merle. *Lyndon: An Oral Biography.* New York: Ballantine Books, 1980.

Milne, David. *America's Rasputin: Walt Rostow and the Vietnam War.* New York: Farrar, Straus and Giroux, 2008.

O'Neill, Tip, with William Novak. *Man of the House: The Life and Political Memoirs of Speaker Tip O'Neill.* New York: Random House, 1987.

Patterson, James T. *Grand Expectations: The United States, 1945–1974.* New York: Oxford University Press, 1996.

Pearlstein, Rick. *Nixonland: The Rise of a President and the Fracturing of America.* New York: Scribner, 2008.

Perkins, Frances. *The Roosevelt I Knew.* New York: Viking Press, 1946.

Peters, Charles. *Five Days in Philadelphia.* New York: PublicAffairs, 2005.

———. *How Washington Really Works.* 4th ed. Reading, Mass.: Addison-Wesley, 1993.

Phillips, Rufus. *Why Vietnam Matters.* Annapolis: Naval Institute Press, 2008.

Prochnau, William. *Once Upon a Distant War: David Halberstam, Neil Sheehan, Peter Arnett—Young Correspondents and Their Early Vietnam Battles.* New York: Vintage Books, 1996.

Public Papers of the Presidents of the United States: Lyndon B. Johnson, 1963–69. 10 vols. Washington, D.C.: U.S. Government Printing Office, 1965–70.

Rapoport, Bernard, as told to Don Carleton. *Being Rapoport: Capitalist with a Conscience.* Austin, Tex.: University of Texas Press, 2002.

Reedy, George. *Lyndon B. Johnson: A Memoir.* New York: Andrews and McMeel, 1982.

Reeves, Richard, *President Kennedy: Profile of Power.* New York: Andrews and McMeel, 1993.

Schlesinger, Arthur M., Jr. *The Age of Roosevelt: The Coming of the New Deal.* Boston: Houghton Mifflin, 1958.

———. *Robert Kennedy and His Times.* Boston: Houghton Mifflin, 1978.

Schulzinger, Robert D. *A Time for War: The United States and Vietnam, 1941–1975.* New York: Oxford University Press, 1997.

Sheehan, Neil. *A Bright Shining Lie: John Paul Vann and America in Vietnam.* New York: Random House, 1988.

Sherwood, Robert E. *Roosevelt and Hopkins: An Intimate History.* New York: Harper and Brothers, 1948.

Shesol, Jeff. *Mutual Contempt: Lyndon Johnson, Robert Kennedy, and the Feud That Defined a Decade.* New York: W. W. Norton, 1997.

Shulman, Bruce J. *Lyndon B. Johnson and American Liberalism: A Brief Biography with Documents.* Boston: Bedford Books, 1995.

Sidey, Hugh. *A Very Personal Presidency: Lyndon Johnson in the White House.* New York: Atheneum, 1968.

Smith, Jean Edward. *FDR*. New York: Random House, 2007.

Sorensen, Ted. *Counselor*. New York: HarperCollins, 2008.

———. *Kennedy*. New York: Harper and Row, 1965.

Stossel, Scott. *Sarge: The Life and Times of Sargent Shriver*. Washington, D.C.: Smithsonian Books, 2004.

Taylor, Nick. *American-Made: The Enduring Legacy of the WPA: When FDR Put the Nation to Work*. New York: Bantam Books, 2008.

Thomas, Evan. *Robert Kennedy: His Life*. New York: Simon and Schuster, 2000.

Updegrove, Mark K. *Second Acts: Presidential Lives and Legacies After the White House*. Guilford, Conn.: The Lyons Press, 2006.

Valenti, Jack. *A Very Human President*. New York: W. W. Norton, 1975.

Vandiver, Frank E. *Shadows of Vietnam: Lyndon Johnson's Wars*. College Station, Tex.: Texas A&M University Press, 1997.

Witcover, Jules. *The Year the Dream Died: Revisiting 1968 in America*. New York: Warner Books, 1997.

Wofford, Harris. *Of Kennedys and Kings: Making Sense of the Sixties*. New York: Farrar, Straus and Giroux, 1980.

Woods, Randall B. *LBJ: Architect of American Ambition*. New York: Free Press, 2006.

Acknowledgments

I suspect that whatever is different about this book comes less from the research and interviews that are the usual tools of the biographer—though they play an important role—and more from the experiences I shared with Lyndon Johnson and those who worked with him.

In 1960, I worked for John Kennedy in the West Virginia presidential primary that turned out to be so critical that he, his brother Robert, and several future members of his White House staff spent the better part of five weeks in the state, much of it in my city and county. I got to know them and, as a result, I came to Washington in April 1961 to serve on the Peace Corps staff as a minor cog in the Kennedy-Johnson administration. In that role, I worked with at least a half dozen future members of Lyndon Johnson's White House staff. This meant that I had friends on each side of the complicated relationship between Lyndon Johnson and the Kennedy brothers. I heard gossip from both camps, including stories about Robert Kennedy's involvement in plots to assassinate Castro and the state of Lyndon Johnson's mental health.

As I began to plan the *Washington Monthly* early in 1967, I got to know several of the most perceptive reporters who had covered or were covering Lyndon Johnson. They included Peter Lisagor, Richard Rovere, Hugh Sidey, and Russell Baker. I already knew Murray Kempton, whose wife worked at the Peace Corps, and Douglas Kiker, an early Peace Corps colleague who left to become the *New York Herald Tribune*'s White House correspondent. The anecdotes and insights about Lyndon Johnson that they shared with me made a valuable contribution to my understanding of him.

Although I was born eighteen years after Lyndon Johnson, I shared many experiences with him. We both acquired chips on our shoulders from the reaction of Yankees to the accents we learned growing up in West Virginia and Texas and the assumption that often seemed to automatically follow, namely that we must be crude, uneducated louts who deserved to be treated with condescension, if not contempt. Johnson and I both lived through the Great Depression, giving us a sympathy for the down-and-out that comes from seeing good and able human beings humiliated by joblessness. And we idolized the man who gave these people hope, Franklin Roosevelt, becoming fervent believers in the New Deal and later in the policy of speaking out against the aggression of Germany, Italy, and Japan and aiding Winston Churchill's Britain in its fight against Hitler.

I first learned about Johnson from the Washington Merry-Go-Round column by Drew Pearson and Robert S. Allen, which was published in the *Charleston Gazette*, among hundreds of other papers. It depicted Johnson as a promising young congressman who admired—and was admired by—Franklin Roosevelt. That was enough for me. I began to follow Johnson's career. Later, through serving first as a page, then as a staffer, and finally as a member of the West Virginia legislature, I learned how hard it was to get liberal bills enacted into law. Thus, I was an awed observer of Johnson's legislative mastery. The Civil Rights Act of 1957, especially given the cautious climate of the 1950s, struck me then, as it does now, even with all its imperfections, as a miraculous accomplishment.

Johnson and I served briefly in World War II, he for six months

and I for eighteen. He had a brief but harrowing combat experience. I had none, but my father had served in the infantry in a long
and brutal battle during World War I. He told of rat-infested
trenches, stinking of human waste and several inches deep in water
or mud, and of men riddled by machine-gun bullets or blown to
pieces by artillery shells. This is what gave me the concern about
ground war that is manifest in this book.

In 1975, my wife and I traded houses with James and Deborah
Fallows, who were living in Austin while she was pursuing her
doctorate at the University of Texas. During that time, I visited
the remarkable Lyndon Baines Johnson Library, the hardscrabble
Hill Country, Johnson's three homes there, and his burial place on
the banks of the Pedernales. We were also able to visit the Alamo.
Few experiences informed my understanding of Lyndon Johnson
more than my amazement at how small the Alamo is, feeling the
desperate plight of the Crocketts and Bowies, realizing the incredible courage and resolve it took for them to die defending it against
repeated attacks by thousands of Mexican soldiers.

For their part in providing all these experiences, I am indebted to
Jim and Debbie, my father, the *Charleston Gazette*, Franklin Roose-
velt, and, above all, my friends in the Kennedy-Johnson administra-
tion and in the Washington press corps. I do not name all the
Kennedy-Johnson staffers because they may not want to be quoted,
but I can acknowledge my considerable debt to four who are now
dead: James C. Thomson Jr., who served as an aide to Chester
Bowles and McGeorge Bundy and who was on the *Washington
Monthly*'s original editorial board; Wilson McCarthy, who was Bill
Moyers's closest political aide during their first year in the White
House; Hayes Redmon, who served as Bill's top assistant on most
other matters; and Redmon's charming wife, Coates, who continued
to work with me at the Peace Corps while her husband was at the
White House and had the delightful frailty of not being able to resist
revealing almost all the inside skinny that came her way.

Although much of this book comes from my memory of
events, I have relied on the many excellent accounts of Johnson's

life—most notably the volumes of Robert Dallek, Robert Caro, Doris Kearns Goodwin, and Randall Woods—and the oral histories produced by Merle Miller, the transcripts of Johnson tapes assembled by Michael Beschloss, and *The Kennedy Tapes* by Ernest R. May and Philip D. Zelikow. I am also indebted to Stanley Karnow's invaluable history of the Vietnam War and the scathing critiques of the American involvement published by David Halberstam and Neil Sheehan. I relied heavily on Nicholas Lemann's *The Promised Land*, Scott Stossel's *Sarge*, and Taylor Branch's two great books about Martin Luther King Jr. and the civil rights movement. Taylor Branch and Robert Dallek have been kind enough to discuss this book with me, as has Jeff Shesol, whose *Mutual Contempt* is indispensable to any serious examination of the relationship between Robert Kennedy and Lyndon Johnson.

I am indebted to Harry McPherson for his memo to Johnson in which he identified with a young Vietnamese who joined the Viet Cong. James Rowe III gave me a copy of the memo his father wrote to Johnson rebuking him for his abusive treatment of his staff, and Mary Margaret Valenti gave me a copy of an unpublished memoir by her late husband, Jack, which contains a detailed account of the July 1965 White House meetings that led to the major escalation of the Vietnam War. Theodore Sorensen provided me with a list of the few people who knew about Robert Kennedy's secret visit to Soviet ambassador Anatoly Dobrynin during the Cuban Missile Crisis—a list on which Lyndon Johnson's name did not appear. The late Robert McNamara, though in declining health, took time to have a lunch and dinner with me during which he discussed both Vietnam and the Cuban Missile Crisis at length and revealed that he had not told Johnson about the Dobrynin visit. I also thank Russell Baker, Joseph Califano, Martin Nolan, Liz Carpenter, Robert and Margy McNamara Pastor, Craig McNamara, Kathleen McNamara, Sam Brown, Peter Kovler, Diane Straus Tucker, Joan Murray, James and Sylvia Symington, Stephen Schlossberg, David Acheson, Sandra McElwaine, Preston Brown, Jon Meacham, John Zentay, and Anthony Essaye for their help.

Finally, my debt to my assistant Joe Dempsey and to my wife, Beth, is simply incalculable. It was the late Arthur Schlesinger Jr. who, while he was general editor of the American Presidents series, asked me to write this book. My affection and esteem for him are great as is my gratitude for his invaluable advice on my book *Five Days in Philadelphia*. Paul Golob, who commissioned that book, is the coeditor of this one along with Sean Wilentz, who succeeded Schlesinger. I could not have had wiser guides.

Index

ABOUT THE AUTHOR

———

CHARLES PETERS is the author of *Five Days in Phila-delphia, How Washington Really Works,* and *Tilting at Windmills,* among other books. He is the founder of the *Washington Monthly,* which he edited for thirty-two years, following a career in politics and government that included serving in the West Virginia legislature, working on John F. Kennedy's 1960 campaign, and helping to launch the Peace Corps. He lives in Washington, D.C.